Toward God

Toward God

The Ancient Wisdom of Western Prayer

Michael Casey

Triumph™ Books
Liguori, Missouri

Published by Triumph™ Books
Liguori, Missouri
An Imprint of Liguori Publications

This edition published 1996 by special arrangement with
HarperCollins*Religious*, a member of the HarperCollins*Publishers*
(Australia) Pty Ltd group.

Library of Congress Cataloging-in-Publication Data

Casey, Michael, monk of Tarrawarra.
    Toward God : the ancient wisdom of Western prayer / Michael
Casey.— Rev.
        p. cm.
    Rev. ed. of: Towards God. 1989.
    Includes bibliographical references.
    ISBN 0-89243-890-8
    1. Prayer—Catholic Church. I. Casey, Michael, monk of
Tarrawarra. Towards God. II. Title.
BV210.2.C368   1996
248.3'2'08822—dc20   95-46093

Copyright © 1989, 1995, by Michael Casey
Printed in the United States of America
First U.S. edition 1996
9 8 7 6 5 4 3 2

CONTENTS

For
Mary, Patrick and John,
Anne, Richard and Robert

PREFACE

This book is a personal statement about prayer. It is not a theological treatise or a historical exposition but an outline of a personal philosophy of Christian life. It is not intended as either normative or complete, but simply as an account of how I feel about prayer at this stage of my life. I hope readers may be led by the text to deeper reflection on their own experience of prayer and on the beliefs and values operative in this area. The reader's final synthesis will, no doubt, be different from mine. I offer my thoughts as one element within an ongoing process of dialogue.

Of course it takes a certain degree of presumption to parade one's deepest thoughts and aspirations through the medium of print, since it is possible to be misunderstood. In my own case, confidence came from two sources. Through many years' apprenticeship under the Fathers of the Western Church, I have come to realize that my own experience of prayer is more typical than I first assumed. From their teaching I have learned the theory of prayer, and I have been constantly guided by them in its practice. Second, I have benefited by being a member of a monastic community, with all the advantages for the life of prayer that this entails. Through these two channels I have come to know and to love the spiritual tradition of the Latin Church, and it is this, above all, I wish to share with my readers.

Although I write from a monastic base, there is nothing esoteric here. My words are directed to anyone interested in penetrating deeper into prayer. The sources of this teaching are the common property of all Christians – and all of us can be instructed by them, whether we have labored long at prayer or whether we are just beginning.

I was conscious, as I wrote, that a number of areas may have been overlooked. I have not spoken much about communal prayer or about the liturgy, nor about the range of human experiences that set the stage for prayer. I may discuss these in future. Here I concentrate on those basic beliefs and values that support an individual's growth in prayerfulness.

This revised version of *Toward God* incorporates a little new material and has given the opportunity for some corrections. I have moved my quotations from *The Cloud of Unknowing* a little closer to modern English, and Chapter 14 is completely new. Again, I express my gratitude to all those who have, by their comments and encouragement, contributed to this book.

Tarrawarra Abbey
Yarra Glen, Victoria,
Australia

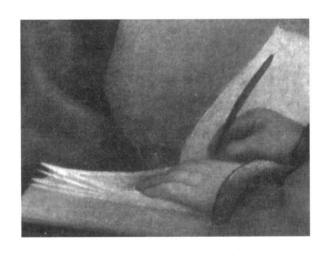

1

TOWARD GOD

In the prologue to Saint John's Gospel, the special character of the Word's relationship to the Father is signalled by the Greek phrase *pros ton Theon*. This is usually translated "The Word was *with* God." There is, however, another element in the expression. The phrase means that the Word was eternally moving *toward* the Father. Far from being a static relationship, the Word is constantly pressing closer and closer to the Father, eternally penetrating more deeply into the heart of God (as Saint John says at the end of the prologue), and being joined to God by the pure passion of the Holy Spirit.

This added nuance is difficult to express in orthodox theological language and, I suppose, that is the main reason why it is commonly passed over. The intricacies of Trinitarian processes may seem a little removed from our daily experience, but it is worth taking the trouble to see how our lives as Christians somehow reproduce the same patterns on a different scale. When the Word became human, Jesus Christ lived the same relationship in a human mode and it is in this relationship that we are called to share. Like the Word, like Jesus in the flesh, we are invited to live our life here on earth as a journey *toward God.*

Throughout the Gospels there are two salient aspects of the identity of Jesus. He is from the Father, sent by God to accomplish a task. Secondly, the human journey of Jesus is one that leads back toward God. It is this movement back toward God that is opened to believers of all generations. In following Jesus, we are shown the way that leads toward the Father. Our life is not aimless; it has a destination. We have not been left to wander in the desert; the Shepherd has come to seek what is lost and bring us home.

Jesus has gone before us. In the words of John 13:1, he has made the crossing from this world toward the Father and summons us to come after him. We will do this definitively when, at the hour of our death, we will have to summon up whatever resources we have in order to cast ourselves into the arms of God. We need to remember, however, that the quality of this supremely personal act is not manufactured at the last moment. It is the fruit of countless small choices made from infancy onward which have given shape to our will. To the extent that our decisions have centered on feeding self we will find it very hard to change course in that awesome hour. On the other hand, if life and providence have taught us to reach beyond self to other persons and to God, then the grace of God will empower us to follow Christ and so enter into glory.

The ultimate truth of human life is that all our searching leads to God. In Saint Augustine's timeless words, "You have made us for yourself [O God] and our hearts are restless until they rest in you." This is something we know about every human being. He or she is made for God; there will always be an incompleteness until a person arrives at God.

When we talk about prayer or contemplation we are really talking about those moments when God enters our life. Drawn by the prompting of the Spirit we are distracted from ordinary occupations, and turn toward God. Something happens then that we are not always aware of. We may not be like Moses, who came down from his encounter with God on Mount Sinai with a face so radiant it could not be looked upon. But each contact with God awakens and quickens some spark deep within us that nothing else can touch. Opening ourselves to God is what makes us come alive.

We were created with an orientation toward God, and so actions that direct us toward God accord with the imperatives of our nature. When we try to live moral lives after the example of Christ, and open our minds and hearts to prayer, we are not simply doing something "religious"; we are fulfilling the most fundamental requirement of our humanity. By God's gift we can turn away from the intangible and immediate, transcend the attractions of sense and image, and stretch forth into the infinite sea of eternity. We can add a new dimension to our human experience.

It is easy to confuse what is true with what is dramatic. If anything religious were to happen to us we would expect it to come upon us like a thunderclap and immediately change everything, without possibility of deferment. I suppose sudden conversions do occur, though I suspect often the suddenness is more apparent than real. What we generally see is the culmination of a process working

underground for years. For ourselves, we do well to surmise that
because we are generally given a reasonably long time on earth, our
journey toward God will be evenly spaced over many decades. We
may not seem to make much progress in any given hour of any given
day; but this is not unexpected. A journey lasting a lifetime cannot
afford to squander its available energies on a few privileged moments.
In fact, like passengers on a small ship crossing the ocean, we cannot
easily gauge the rate of forward movement. Through the years we
ride on tides and currents and are buffeted by waves; often no land is
in sight and the heavens are closed to our gaze; yet we go on.
Everything depends on our being steadfast in holding course, though
there is little at the time to confirm our judgment. The truth becomes
evident only on arrival: despite delays and some wanderings we were,
after all, moving in the direction we wanted to go.

There is a providence of God active in the life of every person.
This is no blueprint which once settled cannot be changed. It is a
patient, paternal, infinitely loving willingness to provide a way from
wherever we are to our Father's house. If we are off course or going
backward or completely stationary, a way can still be plotted. There
is always a way. To put ourselves outside the providence of God
would be like falling off the edge of the earth. It can't happen,
because if we go far enough in the wrong direction we end up within
easy distance of where we should be. Strangely, in letting us wander
off on our own, God often creates through different means the very
virtues we rejected in choosing our own way. It would be wrong to
imagine God as resentful or sullen about having to keep updating our
routes back. In fact, I would not be surprised if the challenge of
ensnaring particularly rebellious human wills appealed to the
Creator's sense of play. Christ certainly showed a special preference
for sinners, and the evangelist Mark keeps reminding us that even the
Apostles were not undeviating in their faith. My own (admittedly
limited) experience with people who have become great friends of
God is that their spiritual capacity is matched by a strong tendency
toward rebellion and riot. Their fidelity is all the greater for being
persistently tested. What matters is arriving at the destination, and
the only way to accomplish it is to keep moving, undeterred by
mistakes and mishaps – whether these come from one's own will,
from powerful forces within, or from outside. It is to be expected that

our journey will veer away from the theoretically correct course. Instead of denying that we have gone wrong, or continually backtracking to the point where we went astray, we must set a new course determined by the real situation and its relation to our destination.

Prayer is our means of taking a sighting, of re-orienting ourselves – by re-establishing contact with our goal. In the presence of God many components of our life fall into perspective and our journey begins to make more sense. We look toward God, conscious that seeking what is unseen corresponds to a very deep stratum of our being. It is not just a bright idea or a fad; it grows from the soil of the heart. Prayer is inseparable from living.

The worst thing we can think about prayer is that it is a trivial exercise – saying a few words or channeling one's thoughts in a particular direction. Authentic prayer is not that. It is usually difficult. This is not because it takes great expertise or is reserved to an elite, but because it takes a lot of courage. To pray well I must first find out where I am. Self-knowledge is never procured cheaply. To pray well I need to face up to realities about myself, that I would prefer to ignore: my anxieties, fears, private griefs, failures, lovelessness, my utter lack of resources. To accept the truth about what I am, as also the truth about other human beings, demands courage. If I do not pray well, it is usually because I lack that kind of courage.

Once I have confronted and accepted – as far as possible – that I am a needy person, the act of turning toward God is relatively easy. It is not faith in God that is hard, but the renunciation of illusory faith in myself. To turn toward God means, first, turning away from whatever is untrue or delusory – no matter how much comfort it brings.

I have never met a man or woman or child without experience of suffering. After the trauma of birth we pass through many difficulties and reversals of fortune before the dread-filled moment of death. We have public and private tragedies, sufferings and anxieties, and our own deep, unspoken fears. This is the stuff of human life. It is precisely the depth of our sense of pain that marks us out as human. Yet in the very worst moment of our suffering, often a spark of life appears. When all appears dead and our mood is wintry, a sign of spring is given us – all the more real and profoundly experienced because we have seen the worst. I suspect it is by passing through such periods that we begin to discover our deeper selves: we make contact with our neediness and find in our hearts a great longing and love for the God who remains unseen. As life goes on and our cumulative sense of this God is strengthened, we begin to desire more intensely and seek God more explicitly. This is the normal way God draws people more deeply into prayer.

There is, however, still a question. Suffering does not always produce prayer. The advent of pain can narrow our horizons, making us concentrate on ourselves and our misery, rather than transcending self and becoming detached from the limited satis-factions human life offers. In that case suffering does not draw us to God but drives us deeper into ourselves and toward despair. Suffering can double: once aware of it, we think about it and worry about its implications.

The effects of suffering are not limited to its immediate consequences. It has impact on life as a whole. Sometimes one needs it in order to grow more tender. As we reap our own harvest of grief, it is hard not to learn compassion. Our love for others is purified: the pain we have experienced makes us less and less willing to hurt anyone else. We become more human.

When life is very difficult, people sometimes lay hold of resources that they never knew they had. The easy-going, self-centered exterior is cast off and a person of heroic stature emerges. Under pressure, false and foolish facades slip away. A new person emerges, or rather the one who has lain dormant these many years, tyrannized by an outward image bearing little resemblance to what was within. Suffering causes the mirror to crack. As the pieces fall away, we see what is hidden behind.

In the culture of the industrialized Western world, it is difficult to accept suffering. We are led to expect that it should not occur. If we lack acceptance or love of self-confidence, perhaps some consumer item will redeem the situation. Like some vast pharmacy, our technological society offers a remedy for almost every ailment. We come to believe it is not right to experience pain. We are encouraged to block it out, to forget our misery, to act "normally." Millions of people walk around pretending to be "normal."

As human beings we are vulnerable. The surest mark of adulthood is the capacity to accept that vulnerability in oneself, and in those one loves. Not to hide from problems but to accept them as part of total reality. One can sit down and talk to them, as it were, trying gently to understand the roots from which they spring. Instead of trying to restrict a problem to a narrow band so that it can be easily grasped and a quick solution devised, it is often wiser, and kinder, to see a negative situation as a symptom of some deeper malaise. This should not cause panic or exaggeration; on the contrary, it should help one see everything in terms of the whole person – myself or another. In time, after much agonizing and resistance, we begin to appreciate the neediness and weakness of every person, and to experience this in love, not in rejection.

This realization is not something desperate, but full of hope. It is a paradox that despair is strongest while we resist the full truth, while we cling to one element of the total situation or to some cherished notion and fight to avoid the onrush of its contradiction. There is a serenity that comes from facing the worst, and a strength that is full of hope. So long as we deny the existence of what we fear, we isolate ourselves from the source of courage. Far from being liberated, we are pressed deeper into dread.

By a strange inversion, only as we experience the extent of our human liabilities do we discover within ourselves the movement toward God called prayer. "The Spirit comes to the aid of our weakness. We do not know how to pray as we ought, but the Spirit intervenes with sighs, deeper than any words" (Romans 8:26). The experience of the Holy Spirit praying within us is inseparable from a sense of our own weakness and incapacity. By the action of the Holy Spirit what is worst in us can give rise to what is best. This is an alchemy we do not comprehend and can never anticipate, no matter how often it happens. God transforms human limitation into something beautiful, taking what is of least value and ennobling it from within. This is properly the work of God. We have only to submit, by suspending judgment about the relative value of things. An earthy image used by the Church Fathers illustrates this point.* A basketful of manure is not valuable on its own, but in the hands of a

---

* The term "Church Fathers" refers to the great pastors, preachers and writers of the first one thousand years of Christianity. Those who figure in this book are discussed briefly in the Appendix, pp. 172–176.

master gardener it is placed around the roots of trees to produce growth.[1] Our sadnesses and pain may not seem worth much, but they are fuel the Holy Spirit kindles into love.

The Word of God has become part of human history. He is one with us in our suffering; we are one with him in journeying toward the Father, in the Spirit. By the mystery of his Ascension, Jesus has passed beyond the limitations of space and time; he is as present now as ever he was in Galilee, though unseen. His immensely tender presence can be sensed sometimes, when other things are not claiming our attention. He is in solidarity with us through all we experience, a hidden source of comfort and challenge inclining us toward his Father. It is not we who have chosen Christ; he has taken the initiative with us.

With him, too, and with us is the vast company of God's friends – Mary, his mother, and all the communion of saints, great and small, famous and unknown, together with the mysteriously active host of angels and those he has called from the four winds to be his people here on earth. We are not alone. Often what we need is mysteriously supplied by one whom we could least expect to be an agent of grace. There is but one journey for human kind: all of us who make it make it together.

Prayer, then, is entering the unseen reality of our lives. It is allowing ourselves to experience the mystery in which we are. Suffering is a door in the wall that daily routines erect around our hearts. Passing through it we begin to understand something of the dark side of human experience, something profound, something a little frightening because it is so large, yet something immensely tender and gentle too.

In bringing us to the reality of our life, prayer also introduces us to the reality of God's life. We are put in touch with the persons of the Holy Trinity, not through words but at a deeper level. We feel that we are from the Father and that our whole life is a journey toward God. We discover a sense of solidarity with the Word, in our being bonded with the person of Jesus and in our union with all the saints. We experience the presence of the Holy Spirit, inciting us to good, turning our thoughts to God, directing our actions, supplying for our weakness and, like a homing beacon for an incoming plane, guiding our steps toward the very heart of God.

Divorced from this global vision, prayer does not make much sense. It seems irrelevant to anyone living without reference to distant horizons, and a burden to those who do not know what to expect from it. Human life is one long movement toward God. Prayer is the moment when we become more aware of the nature of that journey.

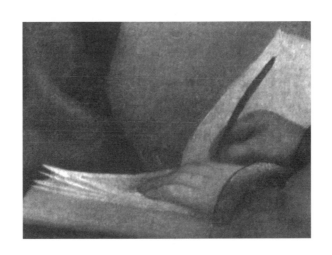

2

THE HUMAN BASIS
OF PRAYER

Discontent is crucial to the emergence of prayer. This may sound a bit grim, but it need not be so. Certainly there is a mood of discontent that is depressive and dispiriting, that paralyzes initiative and retards development. But not all discontent is like that. In fact the sort of negativity described above is often only a phase of a process that, taken as a whole, is creative. It may be discontent with limited opportunities that motivates a person to risk entering a more challenging occupation. It may be discontent with the negative elements in a marriage that causes partners to sit down and work together to improve the situation. It may be dissatisfaction with existing technology that impels an inventor to design a better mousetrap. Contentment, on the other hand, can lead to complacency: getting what one can from what is available with no desire or energy to be creative.

Discontent is often a positive sign, especially when prompted by a glimpse of something better. Measured against a nobler ideal, present reality limps. If the discontent is authentic, it will generate zeal to bring the existing situation into line with the higher vision. A person might realize one day, "This house doesn't have to be such a shack: we can start caring for the garden, gradually renew the paintwork and throw away some of the accumulated junk." Discontent, when strong enough, can start a process, thereby improving morale and giving grounds for hope.

Discontent, then, is a realistic response to a situation lacking perfection. The word closest to it in a religious context is "desire." The Latin term *desiderium* means a lack or defect; the experience of desire is fundamentally a sense of incompleteness. At a very deep level of our spirits, we seem to have a memory of something better. Children born in a refugee camp may be delighted at a poor meal; less so their elders who remember better days. Our memory or intuition of a better state will not allow us to be totally absorbed in what is immediate. The first stage of our questing for the ultimate is dissatisfaction with what is close at hand.

So we become aware of reaching out from the here-and-now into the beyond. In everyday life the real object of our desire is not always visible. Often when our wishes are realized the aura surrounding them quickly dissipates and the ache returns. It is easy to be deluded into thinking some particular thing or experience will satisfy the drive that motivates our search for the Holy Grail, but it is not so. After you get what you want, you don't want it. The human activity of desiring is basic, and only temporarily linked with specific gratifications. It is meant to keep us moving toward the mystery of what lies beyond.

Discontent is the force that makes us search persistently for an answer to our deepest aspirations. The experience of difficulties invites us to turn to God, seeking a strength beyond our habitual reserves. Once our prayer is answered, we can never quite accept again that reality is limited to the comprehensible sphere of human activity. The intense experience of help sought and obtained may pass, but a residue remains. We never quite forget the experience of which the Psalmist wrote: "To the Lord in my tribulation I cried out, and he heard me" (Psalm 120:1). The urgency passes, the anguish fades and the need for God recedes from the foreground of our thoughts. Yet a fragment lodges somewhere.

Progressively, as we learn and re-learn that God is our helper, these isolated experiences begin to coalesce into some shape. We begin to understand vaguely that our need and God's willingness to supply are as much facts of life as the food we eat and the air we breathe. Our view of life is altered by what we have experienced. The deliverance we receive even in minor matters becomes something about which we feel gradually more certain. What began as a function of pain is transformed into an element of faith.

Turning toward God in prayer is now less bound to the immediate experience of hardship and danger. Recognizing our vulnerability we are more inclined to pray in the words of the Our Father, "Deliver us from evil." No longer is our prayer restricted to dealing with actual dangers. We recognize that we are permanently threatened by destructive forces from within our own unconscious, from external mishaps and from the malice of others. "From my secret sins cleanse me, spare your servant from those outside" (Psalm 19:12–13). We have begun to desire a deliverance that is permanent, eternal, beyond the ravages of time.

The prayer of praise and thanksgiving is both a celebration of what has been experienced and an anticipation of what is hoped for in future. The act of praise is more than a judicious comment on the merits of someone or something we admire. To praise is to celebrate, and to celebrate well one must give assent to life as a whole. We admire the wild beauty of nature to the extent that we do not feel threatened by it. A storm at sea, a bushfire or a large animal on the rampage can in fact fill us with awe and admiration – unless we happen to be the target, in which case we flee. Praise of God is possible only in a person deeply convinced of God's love and protection, and experiencing joy and hope at the prospect of the future. Spontaneous celebration presupposes a pervading optimism. True praise is possible only in a heart liberated from fundamental anxiety – because it has faced the worst and found God there.

Using as a springboard the proposition that prayer is based on discontent, it is possible to formulate four general principles of prayer.

1. Prayer is growth in truth

The kind of discontent we have been considering is remarkable for its realism. It is not useless maundering about lost possibilities but a clear-sighted recognition of one's liabilities and (eventually) of the way these may be overcome or at least reduced. In the case of suffering or grief, this means facing the issues squarely and courageously, even though this exposes one to more pain at a time when one seems already tried beyond endurance. Prayer can never be a denial of reality; looking toward God cannot result in untruth. Prayer leads to truth, even when we are unwilling.

The truth we find hardest to accept is that on our own we are resourceless. It is hard for a generation of achievers to accept peacefully the intrinsic weakness of human nature. It is difficult for those who pursue personal integration to be reconciled to the fact that a war between good and evil is being waged within their wills, and that the outcome is by no means assured. It is a burden for those who have come to expect instant gratification to pace themselves to a different rhythm – to appreciate that genuine human growth is spread over a lifetime – so we pass our days aware that we have not arrived. Those who resist prayer are those who cannot accept the progressive dethronement of self. While self triumphs, prayer is impossible.

Yet rampant selfhood is its own enemy. Far from being exaltation of the individual, it is denial. When we recognize our own powerlessness to achieve all we desire, we know that our desires exceed our resources. This is not defective workmanship on God's part, but an indication of our destiny and the means to reach it. We were made for self-transcendence. To pretend otherwise is to live a lie.

2. Prayer is petition

At least implicitly, whenever we pray we look up from our emptiness toward an unseen abundance, and ask to be filled. This may seem to reduce prayer to acquisitiveness. Sometimes prayers are made inappropriately, but in the long term this is no real problem: praying tends to straighten things out. For one who turns toward God in a superstitious way, prayer will not co-operate. The request will echo hollowly without effect – except to undermine the petitioner's faulty faith and lead to crisis so that authentic faith can be brought to birth. It is better to pray as we feel, leaving it to God to sort out what is genuine prayer and what is delusion. Jesus told us forthrightly to ask, to knock and to keep on seeking. He tells us not to hesitate in our prayer, as though discerning whether it is appropriate (Mark 11:23), James 1:6) We are to be confident that our Father is too indulgent to bother about minor slips of form (Matthew 6:8).

Petition is important because it signals our acceptance of incompleteness, and our desire to receive from God what we cannot ourselves supply. It is an expression of faith and confidence in the power and goodness of our Father in heaven, whom we may approach as favored children. Above all, prayer of petition is often symbolic. Sometimes I pray guilelessly for a parking place. This may seem like a frivolous request. To me, it is a real (if minor) need; to try hiding it from my Father would be a denial of the love between us. But there is more at stake, too. Finding a place to park is not very important on a cosmic scale, but my inability to cope with the situation is significant. It is typical of my whole life. When I look toward God and ask for a parking place, I am really laying open before him the messiness of my whole life. Similarly, treating God as a lost property office signals not only my habitual disorderliness but a deeper incompetence. The small events of daily experience provide me with the possibility of asking God for help in their resolution, and also for assistance on a grander scale. What is wonderful is that God seems to be attentive. "When someone begins praying," Archbishop Temple wrote, "coincidences begin happening." Even if I am left in the lurch, I begin to regard that as a gift also. I have been granted so many of my slightest whims that if any request is denied or delayed I cannot now suddenly doubt the goodness of God; it must be my own assessment of the situation that is awry. So I am forced to re-evaluate – and that is a certain gain.

Every request I make of God is a message telling of my neediness, of my trust in God, of my willing dependence and openness to receive. My requests are often foolish, as I am, but God is well able to cope. Even when I pray for others I pray from a sense of my own inability to help. If sometimes I try to rearrange the world to my own liking, I am not rejected but left resourceless until I recognize the presumption that prompted me. Prayer is the one moment in life where we need not fear to express ourselves in all our stupidity and imperfection. God already knows; it is we who need to be informed.

Nor do I think one should fear transforming God into some sort of fairy godmother. Even if we do initially approach God in that way, we will not be allowed to remain long unchallenged in our assumptions. Prayer itself sorts us out if we continue in it. In any case, sometimes it is only by going astray and being corrected that we eventually find the right path.

3. Prayer always leaves us not fully satisfied

Prayer has its origin in a discontent rooted in human neediness, and would probably not continue if this dynamic of dissatisfaction were to cease. In the Our Father we pray that the kingdom of God will come; until that happy day we will remain conscious of imperfection in us and around us. There will always be discontent. Prayer does not do away with our ever-expanding dreams for a fuller life; rather it feeds them. The more we build up a taste for the spiritual world the less satisfied we become with mediocrity and compromise, and with the distance that separates our ideals from our practice. This was dramatized by Saint Paul as the conflict between two forces equally strong, one upward, the other downward. At the end of his reflections, he places in the mouth of one so divided the words, "Miserable human being that I am, who will deliver me from the body of this death?" (Romans 7:24). As experience in the things of God expands, one becomes even less complacent, pained ever more sharply at the irony of experiencing spiritual desires while still subject to temptation and sin.

This sense of inward division fosters within us a longing for heaven. It is not that we hate the world and want nothing more to do with it. It is not that we can visualize what it means to live in God. Rather there develops within us a nostalgia for a "homeland," where all that is noblest and best in us will flower without effort, and all that is ugly and deformed will have fallen away. Our life is a journey that makes sense only on the supposition that we are going somewhere. When it is difficult to keep moving ahead, we need to reanimate our desire. This theme is beautifully developed in a passage by Saint Gregory the Great:

> The present life is but a road by which we advance to our homeland. Because of this, by a secret judgement we are subjected to frequent disturbance so that we do not have more love for the journey than for the destination. Some travellers, whenever they see pleasant fields by the road, contrive to linger there and thus they deviate from the route undertaken in the journey. As long as they are charmed by the beauty of the journey, their steps are slowed. It is for this reason that the Lord makes the path through this world rough for his chosen ones who are on their way toward him. This is so that none may take pleasure in this world's rest or find refreshment in the beauty of the journey and thus prefer to continue the journey for a long time rather than to arrive quickly. It is also to prevent one who finds delight in the journey from forgetting what it was about his homeland that had enkindled his desire.[1]

Prayer operates as a function of our journey toward God. It is successful when it makes us want to continue the journey with greater urgency than before. If it makes us want to stop by the roadside for a picnic and a sleep in the sun, it is not prayer but delusion.

4. Prayer is a school of self-forgetfulness

Prayer is intended to keep us moving, which means constantly saying good-bye to the past. It involves the difficult task of allowing ourselves to be liberated from our burdens. The odd thing is that most of us keep clutching our useless bundles, as if we would cease to exist without them. We must go beyond our past, go beyond ourselves. To settle on a fixed identity at an early age and to refuse to be budged from it is to pass one's days in living death. There is no growth, no life, and no future different from what has gone before. One tends to relive the events of former times – and finds oneself avoided as a bore. Human life is designed as a continual labor of self-transcendence; the past is there to be built upon, not to become a substitute for an unacceptable present.

Prayer is chiefly about the present and the future. It is an important component in our growth because it maintains the pressure to keep expanding our limits – and not accept as final any restriction on our progress. Prayer stops us giving up the struggle when the obstacles seem insuperable. (Last week they may have been, but who knows about next week?) God's perception of us is infinitely more generous than our own; he will not permit us to continue cultivating a self-image that is tawdry and defeatist. He keeps chipping away at any determination to measure our potential by our own resources: he wants us to forget ourself. To us, as to Saint Paul, he says, "My grace is sufficient for you, for power is made perfect in weakness" (2 Corinthians 12:9). And we are invited to reply, "I can do all things in the One who strengthens me" (Philippians 4:13).

The test of authentic prayer is growth: growth in goodness, growth in humanity, greater serenity in living and in facing hardship. Above all genuine contact with God effects a real displacement of self as the center of our existence. Nobody is as totally self-centered as a baby; the process of becoming an adult is a matter of opening doors to allow other persons and realities access. One who has never matured remains substantially fixated on self. In the spiritual sphere, growth allows others to take center stage. In the first place it means giving God scope to act: this is the work of prayer. Less noticeable is a parallel development: genuine prayer opens us out to others. Prayer is not erecting a private chapel and withdrawing from the rest of humanity. It is more like a wedding feast to which we welcome all who cross our path.

A strange thing takes place in prayer. There is a mysterious coupling of our own life with the lives of others – an embrace that includes the whole of humanity. At first, prayer stems from a sense of personal neediness. We never quite escape this feeling, but in penetrating deeper into our indigence we become aware that this need for God is not private property. We are not alone in being without resources: the whole human race cries out to God for redemption. Prayer progressively becomes less a self-centered plea for personal deliverance than a universal cry for help – and for the coming of God's kingdom. The weaknesses and weariness of all are made personal in me; I come to experience them as my own. And when, from the depths of need or grief I turn to God, prayer arises on behalf of all. Of course, I continue to be most aware of my own afflictions and of those closest to me, but as my prayer evolves, it becomes a universal plea to the Creator of all.

And from this widened prayer develops a wider compassion that finds expression in my daily life. Less and less do I see myself as distinct from the pain of others. More and more I find myself assuming part of their burdens. As the years go by, prayer nurtures a sense of identification with the whole human family and produces a more effective love of neighbor than could natural disposition, efforts of will or ascetical practices.

If discontent is the usual starting-point of prayer life, then it is important to come to grips with the hard reality of life – especially its negative components. We need leisure to reflect on our experience whether as individuals, as partners in a marriage or as members of a community. We do not have to accept the facile optimism in our popular culture, that portrays suffering as a minor hitch in the system – of no significance in itself, soon to be ironed out so that things can return to "normal." We do not have to make a fetish of pain or establish ourselves as resident martyrs – but we do need to confront the human reality underneath suffering.

This means first recognizing that complacency is the enemy of both humanity and prayer. This is the point of Jesus' parable about the pharisee and the tax-collector.

> Two men went up into the Temple to pray; one was a pharisee, the other a tax-collector. The pharisee stood and prayed thus to himself: "O God, I thank you because I am not like other human beings. They are grasping and unjust and adulterous, as is this tax-collector. I fast twice a week and give tithes of all that I earn." On the other hand, the tax-collector stood far away, and he was unwilling even to lift up his eyes to heaven. Instead he struck his breast and said: "O God, have pity on me, a sinner." I tell you that it was the tax-collector that went home at rights with God rather than the other one, because those who lift themselves high will be laid low and those who lay themselves low will be lifted up. (Luke 18:10–14)

We see how the pharisee is said to pray "to himself." It is as though his prayer goes nowhere. It does not reach God because he is unwilling to relinquish an inappropriate self-esteem. "Good people" can find prayer hard if they do not confront their own sinfulness. Meanwhile, those whose sinfulness cannot be concealed even from themselves, find prayer comes more readily.

Complacency need not derive from smug self-righteousness. Sometimes it comes from not understanding the extent of one's liabilities. A man may think there is nothing wrong with his marriage, right up to the day he comes home and finds the house empty. A woman may really believe that all she does is for the good of her child, until she reads the psychiatrist's report. When unhappy events shatter complacency both cry out, "Why didn't I figure this out for myself?" Nothing is more difficult than admitting our judgment was in error, and that energies we invested because of it may have been lost. One fears to confront the possibility of a serious mistake, and then compounds pain by not addressing the fear. We cover it and hope things will right themselves. To face the truth about our lives is never easy.

Our minds shrink from recognizing the possibility that our existence is built on sand. It is not surprising that we flee in fright from thinking about life. Without an inner certainty about the direction of the journey, our choices are constantly weighted toward sources of comfort. Disturbing thoughts can be blocked. Football, soap operas and the sex lives of "media personalities" can become more "real" than one's own life and family. And if these do not keep the thoughts from drifting back to challenge us, one can seek relief in drugs and alcohol. By a sustained round of work and play, one can manage to leave no moment for reflection. It *is* possible to evade the warning intuitions, but at a cost.

One never enjoys life while holding the door closed against reality. When we find ourselves anxious or angry or fearful, the object of these negative emotions needs to be faced. Otherwise it will dominate our thoughts and absorb our energies. Then life becomes a sustained effort at avoiding real issues. Rather than securing our own survival, we are using up resources in postponing the inevitable. Life cannot be enjoyed if one is selective in this fashion. If the thing we dread is true, then accepting it gives us vitality, while deferment is deadening. The diagnosis of a terminal illness in a loved one is a shattering experience. Yet to accept it in all its horrific pain means the days that remain can be exploited to the full – and all we desire to say before the final parting can be said. To deny the danger and attempt to carry on as normal deprives us of filling those days with a special love openly expressed. To accept an unpleasant truth about ourselves, an ugliness from deep inside, is very hard. But after acceptance we have the chance to offset its influence. This may not mean an easier life, but certainly a radically freer one. The monster once discovered can be constrained.

Insisting that prayer brings us face to face with our own darkest features may appear depressing or too demanding. I do not deny, of course, that there is a joyous element in prayer, and we will explore this later. But the real problem many people have in prayer comes from the fact that to be authentic, prayer must be grounded on truth. If it is not, it is spurious. Even if it is, it will inevitably have moments of anguish and dread.

Prayer helps us cope with the rigors of truth because we do not face it alone. For one with active faith, awareness of something unpalatable comes packaged with assurances of God's help. Often we can face the worst only when we know a solution is at hand. Prayer reveals our liabilities, but it also reveals the Father who calls us, the Word who accompanies us as we journey, and the Spirit who gives us heart. Prayer means not fleeing from the worst but doing battle with it, empowered now with the strength of God.

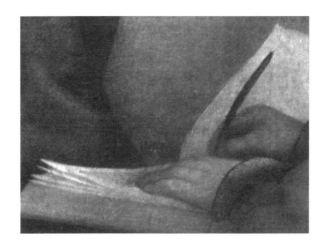

3

GIVEN, NOT ACHIEVED

Prayer is strange in being an activity where no success is possible. There is no perfect prayer – except insofar as it corresponds to one's real situation and represents a total turning toward God. The ecstatic prayer of a mystic is in no way superior to the agonized stumbling of a sinner weighed down with guilt and deformed by a lifetime of estrangement from God. Both attempts represent the upward striving of created nature to find rest in God; both are real, both are "successful." Both remain imperfect, too, because perfection does not belong in this life; it is to be expected in the next. And when God's judgment turns everything upside down and exalts the lowly, who can say which of these prayers has the greater capacity to be raised?

In the previous chapter I stressed the importance of truth as the basis of prayer. Real prayer arises from our actual situation. Here I wish to reflect on the ground of prayer – what it is that causes us to look toward God, especially when we feel oppressed.

A rubber ball held under water submits. Once released, it springs to the surface; and the deeper it is held the more it strains to rise. The human spirit possesses a natural buoyancy. It can be held down by enslavement to the senses, by acquisitiveness and ambition, by anger and violence, or by what the New Testament calls "cares." It can be held down, but its natural tendency remains dynamically oriented toward God. It can never be entirely satisfied until this upward impulse is allowed freedom. To eliminate the divine dimension is to inflict a distortion on one's personality that ultimately results in great harm.

Am I saying that prayer comes naturally? Yes: not that prayer comes easily, but that it does come naturally. All difficulties experienced in prayer are due to our having lost the habit of living in accord with the nature God gave us. We have overlaid our natural tendency toward God with human conventions that enclose us in a narrower sphere, like a bird in a gilded cage. We may forget our call to seek what is unseen. The Western world is tolerant toward religion, which is generally regarded as a good thing – like jogging. If it does you good, go ahead, so long as you don't upset other people. Religion and jogging are seen in our pluralistic society as optional extras. The churches seem not to question this assumption. Much energy is expended demonstrating that religion is a *desirable* optional extra. It will enhance your life. So religion becomes a "product" to be sold, just one of many pathways to individual fulfillment.

This is where we part company with the conventional wisdom of contemporary Western society. It is crucial to an understanding of prayer, and of human nature, to appreciate that we are made with an orientation toward God. We can never be satisfied with this life's range of gratifications. We have been made with a vast capacity for God and for eternal life, so everything else is of relative value, with only relative power to attract our interest and hold our love. We were made for God: to deny this is to distort our self-understanding and guarantee that our growth will not be authentic.

Experience shows that irrespective of what we have achieved and acquired we still have desires. We continue to hanker after something more. Often these desires cannot be fulfilled; sometimes they are self-contradictory. And when we cannot admit our aspirations into consciousness, they find expression elsewhere: in myths, dreams and fantasies.

Fantasies or daydreams have not been studied sufficiently, though they are often highly significant in pinpointing areas of vulnerability within an individual's life. (What is still more interesting is to see the totality of daydreams embodying the cumulative aspirations of the human race.) Usually the daydream is the obverse of life: a person who is hungry fantasizes about food; one who is tired, wet and miserable dreams of a comforting bed. Our fantasies express in graphic form the need we have, though we may not be aware of its full dimensions. The five human priorities commonly manifested in daydreams tell us much about our natural yearnings.

- We yearn to be *invulnerable* and beyond pain. We conjure images of our own place – an environment not alien but familiar and safe, remote from the reach of enemies and those who do not understand. When hurt too often, we long to retreat to a mountain fastness, a desert island – or even a comfortable suburban dwelling.

- Those who belong to the "civilized world" sometimes deep down wonder what it would be like to throw off the trammels of convention and run wild. While appreciating the benefits of rationality, sometimes we would love to be *uninhibited* – give scope to our noble animality, be spontaneous and free, act unreflectively, and fly, unshackled by routine. "If only I had the means, I'd drop everything and make a new start."

- To the extent that one feels unaccepted and misunderstood, one yearns deep down to be *validated* and confirmed. We have a desire to be acclaimed as valuable human beings, even glorified. Freud remarks that young men are particularly prone to hero-fantasies, probably to offset the unheroic character of routine existence. Oddly, some people gain solace by daydreaming about their own funerals, where their worth is vindicated in the eyes of the multitude. If others do not give us recognition, our fantasies contrive it.

- Acceptance, however welcome, is still not enough. We desire *intimacy*. We want to admit others into our space and have access to theirs. And though in daily living we may spend much time and energy keeping others at a distance, we do desire closeness. We cannot survive alone; we need companionship. Frequently, like children with no one to share their company, we conjure up a fictional friend.

- Above all, we desire to be *whole*. Our lives are scattered over disparate moments of space and time. A twentieth-century person travels widely. By the end of a long life, one has made contact with hundreds of other men and women who have since gone their own way. Once they were part of our lives; now they are not, and we are the poorer for it. We sometimes wish the golden moments of life could be gathered in an instant – that we could enjoy the freshness of youth and the mellowness of later years together. How pleasant it would be, as in dreams, to break down the barriers of time and move without restraint. Instead of being divided interiorly and without, our desire is to have life compressed into a single rich experience of now – containing in one moment all those personal energies that are presently fragmented. Then we would be fully alive!

Fantasies can spring from self-pity, but even then they indicate something about human sensibility. Beneath them all is our dissatisfaction with the good things of this life and our consequent longing for heaven. Whether we call it by that name, whether we give it religious connotations or not, we do yearn for a fullness of joy, and for ever. We desire to be invulnerable, without limits to freedom – spontaneous and uninhibited. In fact glory will be ours, the ultimate validation. Communion with God and with those we love will satisfy our needs of intimacy. And all our being will be gathered in one: our hearts will be pure and simple, devoid of duplicity, and our lives and loves will come together in an endless moment of total fulfillment.

Is heaven, then, simply a case of wish-fulfillment? Yes, because no wish of ours will be left unsatisfied. No, because our present hankerings are only the dimmest foreshadowings of what is to come. Our desires point to a void that God will come to fill. Meanwhile even our most spiritual words and hopes are babblings when compared with the reality to come. "Eye has not seen, nor has ear heard, nor has it risen in the human heart: what God has prepared for them that love him" (1 Corinthians 2:9).

Saint Paul puts the question of heaven firmly on the level of faith. In a sense it is easier to believe in God than to believe in heaven. The popular image of heaven – clouds, white nighties and harps – does not enhance its credibility. Yet if there is no heaven, Christian life is meaningless. Saint Paul knew this too: "If for this life only we have hope in Christ, then of all human beings are we the ones most deserving of pity" (1 Corinthians 15:19). Heaven is integral to Christian faith. It is the ultimate incentive to do good and avoid evil. Without it, religion tends to degenerate into private guilts or public images.

Jesus' way was not promulgated as law but as a means to happiness. The beatitudes are not moral aphorisms so much as statements about human nature. The following of Christ is not a moral program but a means of attaining unending happiness. It does not matter, relatively speaking, that we experience hardship and alienation now because "our citizenship is in heaven" (Philippians 3:20). It is the fact that we agree to journey toward the eternal life promised by Christ that gives us our Christian identity.

It is important to scrutinize our own experience for "intimations of immortality" – to confirm that religion and prayer are not additions to our basic humanity, but are its deepest and truest expressions. As mentioned, even the banal reality of daydreams points to a need for God.

Reluctance to admit the intrinsically religious or spiritual aspect of human nature appeared comparatively recently – within the last four hundred years. It advanced with a progressive dehumanization of society from the time of the Industrial Revolution – though its roots are older. Earlier, for more than a thousand years, the Church upheld with vigor and strength the essential spirituality of human nature. Its preaching and practice were based on this belief.

The key concept in the Church's anthropology came from the statement in the Book of Genesis that man and woman were created in God's image (1:27). This is an extraordinary statement from a tradition convinced that God is not bodily. There are several different lines of interpretation. One that gained currency among the Fathers of the Church is the conclusion that between God and human beings there is an innate compatibility. We were created with a capacity for God that is pre-elective: it does not depend on any choice we make but is there as part of our basic humanity. This capacity can be realized or left unsatisfied – that is our choice. But we were made for God, and without God our nature is fundamentally frustrated. As Saint Bernard affirmed:

> God is love and there is nothing in all created things which is able to fill the creature who has been made to God's image except the love which is God. For God alone is greater than the human being.[1]

If the human being is truly in God's image, godliness cannot be alienating. Our leaning toward God is the deepest constitutive element in our personal history – not at all dependent on our capacity to recognize, understand or talk about it. What makes me specifically myself is a unique relationship between God and me. Called into being, I have a "name" that is given to none other. I exist as I am because God's providence has arranged a genetic base and a history into which I am born.

The practical consequences of this philosophy are important. If religion is the assertion of the properly personal elements of our existence, then to promote religion is progressively to put aside whatever is less than personal, whatever is alien or imposed. This is well-expressed by the twelfth-century Cistercian author, William of St Thierry:

> O image of God, recognize your dignity,
>   allow the imprint of your Maker to shine out from you.
> To yourself you may appear mean
>   but in fact you are precious.
> To the extent that you have fallen short
>   of him whose image you are
>   you have become stamped with foreign images.
> But if only you begin to breathe again
>   to live as you were created,
>   if only you accept a discipline of life,
> then you will quickly shed and part company with
>   those adulterous images
>   which are like stains clinging to the surface.[2]

Whatever manner of life we adopt, religion's proper purpose is to scrape off the grime so that the gifts of God can shine with greater clarity.

Prayer is not extrinsic. It is a conscious attempt to identify with our natural tendency toward God. It tries to release our innate buoyant impulse. If a person learning to swim doubts that the body will float naturally, much energy will be used to avoid disaster. Others, convinced of their natural buoyancy, will simply relax, feel supported by the water and enjoy the primal sense of being borne up. Prayer will carry us if we relax and do not struggle against it; if we try to conquer it or control it we will get into difficulties.

However, one does not accidentally drift toward God. Movement comes from a free choice. At some particular stage of life we have to make a deliberate decision to turn toward God, leaving aside any goal that draws us in other directions.

Sometimes a radical turning toward God takes place in early childhood, even before one has clear religious concepts. Perhaps not even the name "God" is used. The experience is one of searching for what is beyond. This may be embodied in a strongly remembered moment, or may be the cumulative result of many small events. But it is real. For some, this experience marks the dawning of reason and the beginning of a sense of identity. It may give an orientation to their whole life. We all know persons stamped from their earliest years as seekers – people in pursuit of the Absolute, who can never take the realities of this world as final. Early life experience gives them a certain cast in thinking about themselves and the world; their way is not tied to abstract or theoretical propositions but is intuitive, universal and unstructured. They may find a faith that embodies, in an approximate way, what they have experienced. They may succeed in integrating what they have experienced so strongly into a personal lifestyle. They may remain always on the fringe, impatient with words or rules that do not mirror what they have "seen." To escape the pain of being different they may repress the experience and live as though nothing happened – to their great impoverishment.

In others there seems to be no memory of being drawn toward a transcendent God during childhood. Whether their background is conventionally religious or not, such people often have in later life a different experience that fulfills the same function. Sometimes, in fact, the experience takes place several times. On each occasion one feels invited to renew and reinforce a commitment to the unseen reality of God. This experience usually goes by the name of *conversion* – a turning away from immediate realities and a desire to seek out something as yet hidden and mysterious. This is no rational process though it may be eminently reasonable. Nor is it merely a decision to improve one's moral behavior, though this may be included in the overall agenda. It is, rather, a secret choice to listen to one's heart and be guided by it into mystery, toward God.

In the Christian Church this moment is symbolized and embodied in the rite of baptism. An interior conversion is externally expressed. The former state of alienation from God is terminated; one becomes a member of a community dedicated to the same lifelong journey toward God. One is raised to the position of son or daughter, a member of the household of God, a sharer in the divine nature.

If baptism is the sign of an interior act of conversion, then what of infant baptism? Here the individual act of turning follows, rather than precedes, the ecclesial event. The grace of the sacrament and the commitment of the parents to the child's Christian education mean that the faith is imparted to the child who later, at one stage or other, must make a personal choice. In many cases the gift is latent: it remains underground till something happens to activate it. In a sense this is true for all of us: we have to keep renewing our faith and opening our hearts to the gift of God given in the sacrament. Our lives are fragmentary, and no decision of ours is irrevocable. God's gift and call are given once, but we cannot fully respond in a single moment; our fuller response must be a lifetime of saying "yes."

The mechanics of conversion and baptism are less important than the result of this dual process. We are established and confirmed in a stable relationship with God – one that does not cease when it slips from our minds. We are established in a *state* of communion with God – at the level of being, not of feeling or consciousness. It is a state of which we sometimes become aware, but it is not restricted to our moments of awareness. Once baptized we *are*, by grace, children of God.

In ordinary relationships, one's bond with others is the result of what happens over many years. It is pleasant for those concerned when one's present experience of a relationship embodies all that was good about our shared past. Unfortunately this does not always happen. Momentary events can obliterate the weight of the years, and we are conscious only of negative feelings between us. But even a quarrel cannot wipe out what has happened between us. Years of love do not evaporate. They remain active and modify the present relationship. A quarrel between lovers is painful because the negative present does not reflect the happenings over the years. Past events can never be denied so successfully that they are erased.

Through baptism, God has made us his children; this can never be undone. We can rebel, or be forgetful or unappreciative, but the gift once given remains. Something has happened between us. This is clearest in the case of an adult acceptance of faith. By God's gift the person is attracted towards the mystery and feels at ease with God. In turning toward God, one experiences a moment of deep acceptance and feels united with God. Whatever happens afterward, this gift of grace remains a reality. The memory of it may be repressed, or driven from one's heart with scorn and hostility. It may be swamped by self-gratification or distorted by an unwell mind. But it remains part of a shared history, God's and one's own. In many cases it is aching to be reactivated, if only the chance arises.

Prayer, then, as the act of turning toward God, is not just an application of energies to one task among many. It fulfills the whole purpose of one's being. It gets us in touch with our deepest reality, penetrating beneath the superficial layers of routine experience to the level of being. We were made for prayer; it is the most human and personal thing we do.

Beautiful expression is given this teaching in a fourteenth-century English treatise on prayer, composed by an unknown author under the title *The Cloud of Unknowing*. With lilting grace, the writer asserts that we were made for contemplation (which he terms "this work") and without it we decline:

> Therefore, do not be surprised that I encourage you to this work. This, as you will hear later, is the work in which human beings would have exercised themselves continually if we had never sinned. For this work were we made and all other things were made to help us in it. It is by this work that we will be restored. On the other hand, if we put off this work we fall deeper and deeper into sin and stray further and further from God. And by continuing in this work alone we rise evermore higher and higher away from sin and nearer and nearer to God.[3]

Prayer is the native environment of a human being; each of us thrives in it. And if by estrangement from it we begin to wilt, it is sufficient to come back to it for the process of restoration to commence. Prayer is the opposite of sin; in it all human ills find an antidote.

Apa Pambo, one of the ancient Desert Fathers, was once questioned by a searcher after truth regarding the means of salvation. He replied, "Find your heart, and you will be saved." He was advising the disciple not to seek external things, but to begin an inner quest. To find one's heart is to penetrate to the deepest level of one's being, unlayering stage by stage all that is unessential. To find one's heart means discovering also that at one's inmost center one is not alone. To find the heart is to find that one is related, drawn outward by nature, conversion and baptism toward God. The heart is our innate sense of God. It is to be our first guide, under grace – aided by the discernment of others and by the church's doctrine. Only the heart can provide us with what we need: direction and energy. Others can tell us what to do, sometimes with marvellous insight. All sorts of emotions can motivate us to act, sometimes with heroic generosity.

GIVEN, NOT ACHIEVED   33

But only the heart can provide us with both, and in a manner surpassing all other resources. What comes from the heart and leads toward God carries unmistakable authority, and there is no rest for the will in pursuing anything else. It is the heart (or conscience) that must show the way, create the environment and supply the energy for the long journey toward ultimate beatitude in communion with God. No rejection of outward helps or structures is implied; but unless teaching and pastoral help relate to one's inner reality, they produce conflict and dissonance. Instead of clarifying our true inner imperatives by separating them from other influences, they cause obscurity.

This is probably why Saint John Climacus insists that it is impossible to teach another person to pray. It is true (as he points out) that nobody can teach the blind to see; but what we can do is encourage those who do have the gift of sight to open their eyes and look. Prayer is not taught; all we can do for one another is offer encouragement and support in recognition of God's gifts. This approach to prayer has important practical consequences which are discussed later. We do not produce prayer. During prayer time we do not attempt to initiate a relationship with God; that relationship already exists. Prayer is an attempt to realize the love that unites us with God, allow it to become more present to us, and give it greater scope to act upon us and to change us. We do not produce prayer. We allow prayer to act. All we can do, if we must do something active, is invest our energies to reduce alternative activities – so that prayer may emerge more freely. (It is a little like weeding a garden to let seedlings sprout unhampered.)

I have already noted that what usually causes prayer to arise spontaneously is negative experience, our sense of limitation, our suffering, our unattached sense of discontent. Such feelings can serve as triggers of prayer – although sometimes they seem like its effect. On occasion we feel a sense of detachment from other satisfactions simply because prayer is already secretly at work within us, educating us to seek fulfillment where it can be found more fully. In other words, the gift of grace will operate if we leave it room, but we are not to expect that it will only act by causing sensations of love, peace, happiness and joy. More often our innate sense of prayer will surface by making us very aware of our weakness.

If an important person happens upon us unexpectedly, we may be suddenly aware that we are not in our best clothes. A sense of unworthiness of this kind during prayer is sometimes the direct effect of the advent of grace in the soul. This is an advance, not a decline. Introduced to a different environment, we feel uncomfortable. When God acts on our hearts to win our attention and draw us more closely to himself, the usual first sensation is not exaltation. Like Simon Peter, when we sense a call we are more likely to fall to our knees and say, "Go away from me, Lord, for I am sinful" (Luke 5:8). This is no self-induced guilt; it is an authentic human response in the presence of mystery.

The passive stance adopted before prayer is not always well-understood. We do not create prayer; it creates us. It is a dynamic relationship, a tendency toward God, operating at a pre-conscious level not under the control of one's will. All we can do is consent to it – or reject it by looking for something else to hold our attention. We cannot shape it or change it; all we can do is submit to it or not. Once again, the author of *The Cloud of Unknowing*:

> To express myself briefly: let this thing deal with you and lead you wherever it like. Let it be the worker and you but the sufferer; look at it briefly then leave it alone. Meddle not with it as though to help it for fear of spilling all. Be the tree and let it be the carpenter. Be the house and let it be the householder dwelling inside. Be blind in this time and cut away all desire for knowledge, for that will hinder you more than it will help. It suffices that you feel yourself stirred pleasantly with something that you do not know – except that in this stirring you have no specific thought of anything under God and that all your desire is nakedly directed towards God.[4]

Prayer is not controlled. We are the ones controlled, called upon to submit to a mysterious inward process, to be carried beyond ourselves without ever knowing clearly what carries us or where we are going.

This is why many people speak of prayer in terms of Christ praying in us, of the Spirit making intercession for us, or of the whole Church calling out to God with our voices. Prayer is an intensely personal act, yet it is not confined within individuality. Prayer is larger than any of us. It is less a question of bringing prayer into our hearts than of bringing our hearts into prayer; not drawing water from the sea to fill a bath, but being immersed in an immense ocean and becoming one with it.

That prayer is predominantly a passive event becomes evident during periods of more intense spiritual growth. There are stages of spiritual development that bring rapid evolution in the depth of prayer. These are spectacularly passive times. While enduring them, one is at a very low level psychologically, beset with internal and external tribulations, and incapable of coping well or even receiving much help or comfort from others. This suffering can be intense: sometimes the only reason the spiritual pursuit is not terminated altogether is that, in God's providence, no alternative presents as attractive. Saint John of the Cross termed these experiences "nights." This is an apposite term because they are characterized by an absence of familiar light and by dread of unimaginable dangers. One thinks of the words of our Lord, "The night comes in which no one can work" (John 9:4). During these times the initiative is wrested almost totally from the individual. Prayer becomes its own governor and sets about re-organizing one's whole life. All one can do is to submit uncomprehendingly, seek to allay the ever-present anxiety, learn to endure and be patient (though stretched beyond one's limits), and do whatever seems right, moment by moment. Although they may feel as purposeful as polishing brassware on the *Titanic*, these little acts of fidelity are very significant. They are like signals of love sent out under impossible conditions, and all the more valuable because of it.

We are passive in prayer because prayer itself is active. Prayer cannot be measured on a scale of success and failure because it is God's work – and God always succeeds. When we believe we have failed at prayer, it is because we decided what shape our prayer should have, and are now frustrated that there is nothing we can do to implement our ambition. Prayer is nothing more or less than the interior action of the Trinity at the level of being. This we cannot control; we can only reverently submit.

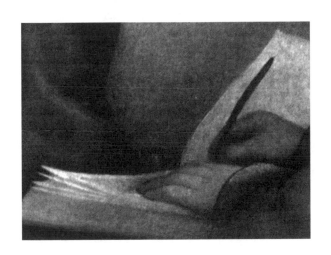

4

A BLIND FEELING
UNTO GOD

P rayer is not a matter of actively thinking about God. It does have a mental component – one of its tasks is to re-form and re-educate our thoughts – but it is not primarily a work of the mind. Efforts to conjure up words, concepts or images are not good beginnings. Its source is an act of love and desire that wells up from the heart. The contents of the mind during prayer spring from the will.

What we *can* do is to create an empty space in our consciousness, and put other considerations aside for the time being so that we can be shaped by whatever comes from the heart. This is easier said than done. As soon as we begin making room for prayer, all sorts of other things begin to crowd in – memories of unprocessed events in one's daily life, emotions that have been triggered and not fully worked through, plans for future projects. These constitute the first wave of attack. When these are repelled we are assailed by others: more distant memories demanding an emotional response: bitterness or anger, or an alienating sense of false comfort. We may begin to observe ourselves at prayer – and derive some entertainment from doing so. Having overcome these distractions we may be almost ready to get started – when we are overwhelmed by a strong sense of boredom or restlessness, or subjected to a barrage of frivolity. And if we do manage to start, it does not seem long before our attention wanes and the process begins all over again. At a later stage we will discuss the practical resolution of such difficulties in prayer. What is important here is simply to appreciate that prayer demands a certain stillness of mind and silence of thoughts. It is not much helped by "wild, wanton wits," to use the expression of *The Cloud of Unknowing*. They are already too active. We need a quiet mind because prayer is subtle. Though there are exceptions, God's presence is not usually felt through the earthquake or the fire, but through the murmuring voice of a gentle breeze (1 Kings 19:11–13).

When, with great effort, we have cleared a space and become empty, attentive, receptive and expectant, prayer eventually asserts itself. The period of preparation is over; real prayer now begins. And prayer does not begin without our knowing it. It may be true, as Saint Antony of Egypt is reported as saying, that "prayer is not perfect if the monk is aware either of himself or of the content of his prayer."[1] But he *is* aware that he is praying or, rather, that prayer is taking place. The experience is not blankness through and through. Nothing may be happening at the level of sense or understanding, but at the level of spirit the one who is praying knows when prayer is kindled.

Prayer does not take place without feeling. But what do we feel? Under the microscope it disappears. There is no hint of the fluffy feelings that may have marked our first steps in the spiritual life. It is infinitely more subtle – something that comes from the heart and transfigures one's sensibility; no mere fluttering of outward emotion. As the author of *The Cloud of Unknowing* wrote, "Look that your stirrings ... come from within, of abundance of love and devotion and not from without, by windows of your bodily wits."[2]

But what is actually felt? Perhaps peace, perhaps a feeling of deep contentment with my lack of peace. Sometimes it is the repetition of Peter's prayer on the Mount of Transfiguration, "Lord it is good to be here" (Matthew 17:4). At other times I seem to hear with dread the words Jesus addressed to his mother, "what bond is there between you and me?" (John 2:4). At times I may be aware of a burgeoning sense of wonder, awe and reverence, of a silence where any word would be intrusive, and a stillness forbids the slightest movement. At other times I may be restless and bored – fragmented, disgruntled and rebellious. Sometimes I feel drawn beyond the shallows into a boundless ocean; at other times it is like being dumped by a rogue wave, and dragged across a gritty beach. In prayer, too, I become conscious of my shoddiness. There is a sense of sin, an impassioned cry for mercy, an ardent plea for the resolution of human misery, even a shuddering sigh an observer might mistake for the histrionics of despair. Sometimes there is no sense at all, just a very deep impression that one's soul is being nourished. The feeling of prayer varies from day to day and from person to person. It cannot be predicted or produced. It has no visible object nor does it come in any characteristic form; it is blind and naked and very deep. But it *is* experienced.

When discussing the feeling quality of prayer, it is hard to avoid extremes. One should neither make prayer into a "heartless" exercise of rationality, buttressing moral behavior and enhancing theological thought, nor reduce it to the level of sentimental religion. Prayer has a feeling component, but the feeling is not always positive. Emptiness, guilt and dread may serve an irreplaceable function in our prayer, and as such are good. We do not have to banish them and seek evenness of spirit by blanking out our minds; we do not have to turn aside from them because they render no comfort. We must attend to these states of mind because they intend our good. They are the harbingers of God. The negative feelings that arise during prayer exist only in view of the arrival of the King. Otherwise the change they urge would be pointless. It is in hope of God's coming that we move gladly to remedy what is defective.

In our sensate culture there is evidence that we are becoming unfeeling people. Our feelings have been exploited too often by the organs of mass communication for us to trust them completely. After much violence and drama on television we fail to be shocked or to take action when others suffer. I remember being sad hearing a small boy describe his first flight on an airliner. He was so blasé. Perhaps he was trying to conceal his genuine excitement, but it seemed he had lived through the scene so often on television that the real experience lacked power to move him. No wonder many in his generation pursue hyperstimulation through drugs, or massive volumes of sound, or risk-taking. Our feelings have been ravaged and trivialized: the outer frontiers of sense are often reached and sometimes crossed, but the inner regions remain unexplored. No wonder people are dubious when one speaks of prayer as a feeling. It *is* a feeling, but not of the same order as alcohol, sex or the excitement of a football game.

Those whose thought patterns do not reach back beyond the sixteenth century are likewise suspicious of feeling. For them the body and soul are two separate realities: they are usually at war and for safety's sake should be kept apart. In fact such a view would be anathema to Doctors of the Church such as Saint Thomas Aquinas. Still, some of our contemporaries doubt that there is a role for body and feelings in prayer. They may speak about *mental* prayer and wax lyrical about moving beyond feelings, but they leave the impression that praying is a passing into neutral space where joy and fear are equally excluded. They admit no passion in prayer – at least for those who are advanced.

I cannot believe this is so. If my spirit sings, my body will dance. Of course, it is a subtle melody, and a long apprenticeship is required to learn even rudimentary steps. We will sometimes mistake our grosser emotions for what is fine and spiritual. But overall it is unimportant that we sometimes mistake the origins of our feelings. A few minor errors never hurt anyone; but to banish feeling from prayer is a major distortion – and a life sentence to prayerlessness if God did not intervene. To experience a void is not to be unfeeling; it is to make contact with an inner dread. To cocoon this dread and remain aloof from it is to ensure that its task is not done. It remains hidden, unrecognized but still potent. While dread is resisted, so are all the good things, ready to come in its train. When we shut ourselves off from the heart, genuine prayer ceases. We are left to fill in time as best we can, juggling thoughts or suppressing distractions. Perhaps we even develop a knack of emptying the mind and so finding peace. But prayer is excluded until we unbar the doors, face the dread and find in it a messenger of love. A common reason why prayer stops is that one has begun to avoid the negative experience it brings.

When a person is subject to long spells of "feelinglessness" while attempting to pray, some of the following factors may be involved:

- We may be using inappropriate practices – methods of prayer unsuitable to our present state. There may be an inadequate notion of what is involved in prayer, for example, and we feel obliged to keep up a contrived stream of conversation with God, instead of simply being quiet and allowing him to act on our heart.

- We may have ceased trying, and attempts to pray may be little more than efforts to conceal the fact that the relationship with God has broken down. The predominant pattern of prayer becomes pious somnolence – a kind of quietism that demands no effort and involves no challenge. Very often other concerns erode the time allocated to prayer so that eventually, if other factors do not intervene, prayer is left aside for long periods, and may even be abandoned altogether.

- As already mentioned, prayer tends to become feelingless when we refuse to face up to negative feelings and their possible significance. Even the most powerful dread is not unlimited; to uncover its extent is to discover its limitation, and with that limitation the element of hope. Unfaced, even the smallest problem becomes immense; it blots out sun, moon and stars, and no comfort can be had. A coward dies a thousand times, instead of once.

• Because our attitude to God is expressed in our behavior, prayer can be paralyzed by some specific aberration in our daily life. Here one has to be precise. Something specific is at issue – not vague, unattached feelings of guilt or regret over past actions and omissions. Nor am I suggesting, for example, that prayer will be impossible until all our current sins cease. That would leave us all stranded. On the contrary, prayer cohabits quite happily with sin. What it cannot abide is failure to recognize sin. Efforts to excuse ourselves and rationalize our behavior effectively prevent prayer; sin admitted and confessed renews our sense of dependence on God and fuels our prayer.

• Prayer changes as it develops – and frequently we experience times of being caught wrong-footed. This is something we have to get used to. There are, however, one or two times in life when prayer changes direction substantially. This causes us a great deal of confusion, and nobody seems to be of much help. There are many individual variants of such an experience, but Saint John of the Cross thought the options facing us can be reduced to three:

(i)   We abandon the practice of prayer, altogether, or allow it to slip away unchallenged.

(ii)   We decide it is a matter of "toughing it out," so we rigidly continue doing things that used to work, closing our eyes to the fact that at the moment they seem to produce no worthwhile result.

(iii)   We submit ourselves uncomprehendingly to the process, allowing it full scope to change us. We combat our anxiety as best we can and, without looking back, learn to trust what God is accomplishing.

If we choose the first option, prayer ceases to be an issue. If we choose the second, we condemn ourselves to a spell of feelinglessness until forced to re-assess our situation. If we follow the third course, we pass through a stage of great anguish and rapid growth – and after some months or years we find rest.

The absence of feeling that many experience in prayer is a complex condition and not susceptible to easy diagnosis. Here it is enough to note that often it is unnecessary, and that it is something to be combated.

The Fathers of the Western Church took for granted that prayer involved feeling. The expression *affectus cordis* (the feeling of the heart) was current in Latin spirituality. Those who followed Augustine stressed the role of spiritual delight *(delectatio)* in detaching a person from worldly gratifications and bonding the individual to God. The experience of prayer was often described in words like *dulcedo* – which we hesitate to translate because spurious prayer books from the seventeenth century and later have made "sweetness" so saccharine. Prayer was often linked with desire for God, with all the manifold emotions implied by desire. Even that sober source, the Rule of Saint Benedict, defines prayer as an outstretching of the heart, *intentio cordis*. In many ways the thirteenth-century saint, Gertrude of Helfta, represents a peak in this tradition: sober and doctrinally sound, yet lyrical and passionate.

The theme of compunction of heart is integral to this tradition. In current language "compunction" is a synonym for regret or sorrow – essentially a negative attitude regarding some action of ours, probably in the past. In the spiritual tradition it has a wider scope, implying strong feeling. The word *compunctio* points to an experience of being pricked or punctured, a sharply stimulating experience rather than a depressing one. Compunction in this sense is an arousal, an awakening. The experience may be an unpleasant awakening, but still an incitement to activity – not to a sinking sense of grief or guilt.

The experience may in fact be positive or negative. "There are two types of compunction," says Saint Bernard, "One is grief for many excesses, the other is a celebration for the divine gifts."[3] Saint Gregory the Great had earlier developed this same point:

> There are two main types of compunction. First the soul thirsting for God is pierced by fear and afterwards by love. In the beginning, the soul is moved to tears at the remembrance of its evil deeds, and it fears the prospect of eternal punishment. But when, after a long and anxious experience of pain, this fear works itself out, then is born in the soul a calmness coming from the assurance of

forgiveness and so the soul begins to be inflamed with love for
heavenly joys. The one who previously wept at the prospect of being
led to punishment, now begins to weep most bitterly because of
being so far from the kingdom. For the mind contemplates the
choirs of angels, the community of the blessed spirits and the
splendor of the unending vision of God and it becomes still more
downcast at being separated from these eternal goods than it was
when it wept out of fear of unending evils. For it is a fact that when
the compunction of fear has become complete, then it draws the
soul into the compunction of love.[4]

Compunction is a strong feeling that wakens the spirit from its
habitual torpor and directs it toward God. In the words of Saint John
Cassian, it is something "by which the mind is inflamed and set alight
and incited to pure and most fervent prayers."[5] The saint provides
examples of occasions that can have this effect: the beauty of
psalmody (which was a significant factor in the long process of Saint
Augustine's conversion), the teaching of a holy person, the death of a
loved one, the recollection of past negligence. Positive or negative, the
experience has the result of arousing the spirit.

The compunction of love or joy is more strongly emphasized in
the West than in the East. Saint John Cassian thinks it is contagious;
through a receptive heart joy finds entry to the world:

It often happens that because of the unspeakable joy and great
enthusiasm of spirit, the fruit of such saving compunction is to
burst forth in cries of unbearable and unmeasurable joy. The
result is that the great happiness of heart and the feeling of
exaltation penetrate even to the cell of the neighbouring monk.[6]

In the West, as in the East, compunction is often associated with
tears, *compunctio lacrimarum*. This is a tricky area, as Cassian
noted, because tears can be faked, even unknowingly. Here, as
elsewhere, it makes good sense not to be too worried about possible
deviations. The important thing is to become tender-hearted in the
presence of God, and not fear to be acted upon and moved in our
prayer. If we are deluded, God will cause us to be enlightened; and in
any case our common sense will eventually let us know if we are off
the track. The Fathers often compared tears to a renewal of our
baptism, washing away sin and expressing our longing to be one with

God. Genuine tears are generally sober and discreet, more likely to take place in secret than in the market-place. They occur spontaneously and express a deep "feelingful" prayer. Often they produce a sense of relief in one's body proportionate to the anxiety one previously felt.

Prayer is feelingful, though the origin of the feeling is inward, not external. The experience can be very strong, but leaves no inverse aftertaste as externally induced feelings often do. The feeling itself is blind and naked, directed to no clearly discernible object. Prayer simultaneously illuminates both the good and the evil within us. It is not the experience of positive or negative emotions that matters but whether we become sensitive and responsive to the action of God. The function of feelings, positive or negative, is twofold:

- They counterbalance the felt attractions that might prevent or retard our turning to God. (This is a case of fighting fire with fire.)
- They serve as an incentive to do good and avoid evil. A person who *feels* called by God will be motivated to accept many hardships that would otherwise seem unbearable. The feeling provides both energy and direction.

There are dangers in giving too much emphasis to feeling, which needs to be governed by reason, sound teaching and a formed conscience. But "governed" does not mean "suppressed." We are not stoics, but followers of the incarnate Son of God, who became like us in all things. He grieved, wept and rejoiced in the Holy Spirit. He was angry, shuddered in dread at the prospect of his passion and groaned in abandonment at its height. To deny feeling is ultimately to deny Christ. It seems to imply that there is another way of moving toward God apart from being human. Perhaps there is – but I, for one, don't wish to take it.

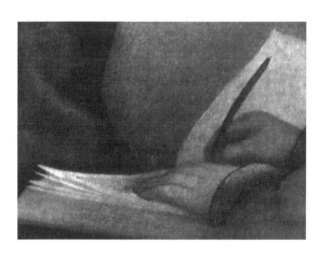

5

THE GIFT OF TIME

"Nothing is more precious than time," writes the author of *The Cloud of Unknowing*.[1] So time is something specially valuable to be offered to God in testimony of our love. Time given to God is time withdrawn from other activities. This means that if I am an achiever, I will achieve less. If I am self-indulgent, I will be less gratified. If I thrive on human contact, I will have to learn a measure of solitude. Time given to God is time not available for self.

This is a hard teaching, both in theory and in practice. For instance, I hope I am doing something good in writing this book. I am obscurely conscious that God is present with me as I write. I may occasionally interrupt the task with prayer. Yet to pray from the heart I need to leave work aside and give myself fully to this something-else-that-seems-like-nothing-at-all. Instead of continuing to pile up pages of text, I cease production. Overall, my active contribution to the work is lessened because I withdraw some time and energy from it and offer them to God.

But, a generous reader may remark, "Such periods of non-engagement in the task add quality to the final product." This may be so; one hopes it is true. But making this a reason destroys the value of the gift. (Money spent on flowers does not repair the roof; a relationship may be enhanced but the rain still comes in.) I would feel I was cheating if my gift were only an apparent one. Time spent in prayer is time lost to temporal gain. It is bread cast onto the waters of eternity.

Contemporary proponents of prayer often recommend it as a useful human activity. They enumerate the *fruits of* prayer: it will bring inner peace and lower my blood pressure; it will help me to understand God's plan and reform my chaotic life. One hears it said that if one practiced prayer conscientiously for a few months, problems would begin to disappear. Prayer has fallen into the hands of self-improvers.

I do not deny that prayer does one good. As I think back over the years it is evident that when prayer receded, problems tended to multiply. Prayer has served me well, but I do not wish to come to prayer for my own enrichment. It is not for fear that I shall be sent emptier away, but because prayer is first and foremost a giving of myself, empowered by grace. In particular it is a giving of my time. I cannot, at this moment, think of a greater favor than the gift of offering myself to God. Other benefits, even those greatly needed or desired, seem less important.

There are times in everyone's life when prayer imposes itself – such as when affliction or anguish breach the boundaries of ordinary consciousness and prayer surges through. On such occasions prayer looks after itself. In a sense there are no problems, it simply happens.

At other times there may be an inward attraction to prayer and nothing more. The occasion for quiet responsiveness is not given, but we must construct it for ourselves. This may mean rewriting the script for the day.

Those who have travelled in an Islamic country have been impressed by the instant obedience many render to the *mu'adhdhin's* summons to pray. What is impressive, despite a possibility of mere formalism, is the willingness to take time out for religious practice. It is this sense of disinterested dedication that must characterize our own efforts to pray.

We need to become ever more sensitive to the call to prayer, be it external or inward. Our divine adoption means that we are in a continuous relationship with God at the level of being. For the most part we are unaware of this. So we need to listen closely, especially if we find it difficult to distinguish God's footsteps among the welter of interior noises.

The Cloud of Unknowing calls the interior invitations to prayer "stirrings." From time to time God's presence is felt within us and we are invited to respond. Such incidents occur unpredictably and without preparation – in a pause between tasks, as a background to other activities or in a time of leisure. They may burst into consciousness, making it difficult to continue whatever we were doing. They may even arouse us from sleep. In an obscure and undefined way we become aware that our whole self is being drawn toward God in a manner fundamentally independent of our conscious willing.

The bubbles in a glass of champagne cling tenaciously to the side of the glass for a long time. Suddenly and without warning, one detaches itself and saunters towards the surface. Sometimes the inward movement of grace follows the same pattern. It is there; it becomes active unexpectedly and then is gone. Much depends on our making the most of such privileged moments. If we simply ignore them – we gradually become desensitized to spiritual reality. These simple summonses to prayer defy rational analysis and elude all attempts to structure them. All we can do is allow them to influence us.

We need to be able to distinguish such stirrings from other interior happenings. This is an intuitive process. It is difficult if we have not built up an experiential capacity to recognize the action of God. At first one must pause and examine the signs closely. Later, recognition of them becomes more immediate. (It is a little like meeting someone at a crowded airport: if we do not know the person well we may attempt a number of mistaken identifications or be confused by the slightest change in the person's outward appearance. With someone familiar, recognition is instantaneous – despite changes in clothing or hairstyle.) In spiritual discernment, a long prayer history helps us recognize God's style. Often we can tell instinctively what comes from God and what from other sources. But this aptitude presupposes prolonged interaction. What is to be done in the meantime?

Our capacity to respond to the stirrings of grace and our willingness to devote regular periods of time to prayer generally grow together. Although unexciting, regularity is important if one is to develop sensitivity to things of the spirit. Dom John Chapman puts this well in one of his spiritual letters:

> The only way to pray is to pray; and the way to pray well is to pray much. If one has no time for this, then one must at least pray regularly. But the less one prays, the worse it goes.[2]

In Western society, where spontaneity is valued, regularity is less prized – though many of the most important human actions take place regularly. If we believe prayer is a significant factor in human behavior or, more personally, if we feel ourselves attracted to prayer, the only practicable course is to allocate to it a slot in the cycle of our lives.

So we must examine our use of time. If our days follow no pattern, it may be necessary to look at a unit of a week. Spreading it out in front of me I ask myself how can I find time to give to God? Probably I will have to experiment a little before finding a blend of spiritual activities that suit the available times and also sit harmoniously with the rest of my life. We need also to build in a certain measure of flexibility, to accommodate the variation in our weeks and allow for changes within ourselves.

Whether we pray or not depends largely on this willingness to organize our lives. It is love of God that inspires this organizing zeal, just as it is often indifference or laziness that resists it. Time is precious and so many things clamor for attention that we will not get around to our spiritual needs unless we arrange a vacant space in which to do nothing else.

As in many other matters, getting started is difficult. Here it is more than a question of overcoming inertia. We are dealing with two different orders of things. Often physical hardship can be endured because the body knows from memory that it may lead to something good. Prayer is not like this. There is not merely question of surmounting an initial barrier, but of consenting to live from a whole different standpoint, displacing self as the cardinal point of life and submitting to be governed by the will of God. Prayer is not just dialogue; it is the first stage of surrender.

Saint Gregory the Great explains the point:

> There is a great difference, dear brothers, between the pleasures of the body and those of the heart. Bodily pleasures set alight a strong desire when they are not possessed, but one who has them and partakes of them, becomes satiated and tires of them. On the other hand, spiritual pleasures are tiresome when they are not possessed, when they are possessed they cause even greater desire. The one who partakes of them hungers for more, and the more one eats the hungrier one becomes. In carnal pleasures the appetite causes satiety and satiety generates dissatisfaction. In spiritual pleasures, on the other hand, when the appetite gives birth to satiety, satiety then gives birth to even greater appetite. Spiritual delights increase the extent of desire in the mind, even while they satisfy the appetite for them. The more one recognizes the taste of such things, the more one recognizes what it is that one loves so strongly. We cannot love what we do not have because this

would involve not having experienced the taste … You cannot love God's sweetness if you have never tasted it. Rather, embrace the food of life with the palate of the heart so that, having made trial of his sweetness, you may be empowered to love.[3]

One's willingness to pray is confirmed if one perseveres in prayer, but beginning and persevering are still difficult. While "one who knows perfectly the sweetness of the heavenly life, happily leaves behind everything previously loved on earth," one who has not yet attained that degree of perfection finds the most sincere resolutions eroded by doubt and lack of interest.[4] So the desire to pray needs to be supported at a practical level. There are too many urgencies, imagined and actual, that can lead us to defer prayer. We need every help we can get.

I can sympathize with those who say it is not possible to do much about prayer because daily events are too unpredictable. But I wonder if they are being completely honest with themselves. What may be lacking is not the opportunity to pray but the desire and will to pray – and that poses different problems. A routine of prayer has to be flexible if it is not to crack under the strain of reality. Structure does not have to be experienced as imposition. It can be liberating. It can enable us to insert into our life something we want included, without having to go through the drama of decision-making on each occasion. We operate on automatic pilot, as it were. (I imagine half the joggers in the park this morning needed no deliberate choice to get out of bed and to start running. They made the choice some time ago to include this activity as part of their day. They may grumble about today's particular difficulties, but they do not judge the value of the project by a single session. It is the cumulative effect over months that matters.) One does make adjustments as time goes by, on the understanding that there was nothing wrong with the original decision – all it needs is a little fine tuning. Flexibility of structure fits well with prayer.

Prayer need not take as long as jogging. We may wish to begin very simply. The oldest suggestion we Christians have comes from the *Didache*, or *The Teaching of the Twelve Apostles*, a work that made its appearance some time before 150 A.D. The author recommends the saying of the Lord's Prayer three times each day.[5] By my calculation, the Lord's Prayer can be said quietly and reverently in about 30 seconds. It is hard to believe someone is so busy that a minute and a half cannot be found for prayer. Nor is this gift so meager as to be unacceptable to God. There are times in the lives of most of us when we can scarcely manage more than that. Even the smallness of our offering is eloquent. Like the widow's mite, it may be all we have (Mark 12:41–44). The gesture expresses our desire to give, and at the same time underlines our paucity of means. Moreover, prayer is prayer, no matter how limited in scope. It is a wedge that will, in time, open our heart wider to the divine reality. Its narrow edge allows it to penetrate more easily. Better to start with a little and upgrade ever so slowly, than to begin boldly and find it impossible to maintain one's pace. The life of prayer is more a marathon than a sprint.

Even a couple of minutes spent each day in prayer and a couple of minutes reflecting on the New Testament is a worthwhile way to begin – or to come back to prayer if we have drifted away. Curiously, once we determine to make these few moments available, storms of resistance will appear. We who fritter away hours without regret find it hard to drag ourselves away for a few moments. To write a book about prayer is not so difficult, but actually to pray – that is another story. Perhaps the fact that we repeatedly resist prayer is an indication that the question is not one of finding time for prayer, but of our willingness to face up to the reality prayer brings with it.

In my experience it is a help to have some sort of structure or routine that jollies us along into prayer before our objections get the upper hand. To pray on rising and retiring and at noon seems important even if the prayer is brief. Prayer before and after meals can be meaningful, even privately done. A few minutes' relaxed and thoughtful contact with the Gospels can help counterbalance our daily diet of half-truths and mistaken values. Celebrating the Lord's Day and sharing the Eucharist in memory of him can be important elements in structuring our week according to God.

On these simple foundations we can build as the attraction of grace moves us. We may find room for greater quantity and variety in our prayer. The rosary or other set prayers may come to mean much. We may find spiritual renewal in regular sessions of quiet meditation. We may grow to love the Psalms, and season our day with segments from the church's prayer, the Liturgy of the Hours. All of these will help strengthen us for the encounter and lead us toward God. Without our knowing it, the divine dimension begins to assume greater importance and we find ourselves being led deeper and deeper into prayer. Not much outward change may be visible, though we may grow gentler and more human, more accepting of our own limitations and more understanding of others. Prayer may come to assume a natural and unforced role in our way of dealing with life. There will still be times of crisis for us and for those we love, but the unseen strength of prayer will be felt. We may experience suffering, grief and the bitterness of regret; these need not destroy our prayer but can purify it and make it whole. Not that we have reason ever to feel smug or self-assured; without being able to explain it, we simply feel drawn to continue attempting prayer, confident that good will come from it. And though we never know what to expect, we keep coming back, knowing that all we have to do is start the process as painlessly as possible, and then get out of the way and let God take over.

Getting started is always a problem, especially if we have allowed prayer to lapse. And special difficulties arise when changes are called for on an external level, or when we need the co-operation of others. Most of us are a little embarrassed if others know we are praying or reading the Scriptures – or if we are doing something semi-public like resuming or intensifying our sacramental life. It is not so much that we fear ridicule, but that we are conscious that our own lives are no great advertisement for religion. Strangely, many of us are prevented from living a more spiritual life because of our own honesty. We are held back by a sense of unworthiness. We do not want to seem better than we are, so we resist God's grace calling us to make a new start.

Because prayer is often regarded as solitary communion with God, many find it hard to take the initiative of introducing prayer into a more communal sphere. Many good Christian families never pray together except at church, although all may pray alone. Many friendships between Christians have never been seasoned by common prayer. It is as though one sector of life is excluded from mutual sharing.

Prayer is a necessary expression of our human need for God: it is at once solitary and social. Any interpersonal relationship that ignores spirituality is liable to founder on superficiality. Somehow the wall of embarrassment that surrounds our interior life needs to be breached so that this deepest aspect of our being can be shared with those we love. The forms of such prayer will have to be discussed by those involved; sometimes a partner or a family member will resist practices another finds helpful. Prudence, tact and respect for others' sensibilities must prevail.

The task of bringing prayer into our environment is not limited to those who are, in God's providence, good practicing Christians. It applies equally to those who, in God's providence, have become unchurched and to those who feel rejected by God because their domestic situation is officially irregular. I think here of remarried, unmarried and homosexual couples. No matter what our personal history or present status, as human beings we retain our need for God, and thus our need for prayer. God's grace is eminently realistic. It touches us wherever we are and asks no more of us than we can give at the moment. We do not have to banish God from our lives because circumstances have alienated us from the church. We give what we can and open the door as far as we are able. God works with us as we are.

Whether alone or with others, prayer is always a gesture of dedication. We offer our time to God; we keep aside at least a portion of our lives specially. We allow God freedom to act upon our hearts. For God's sake we renounce our own expectations: we come to prayer to give rather than to obtain, recognizing that our giving is also God's gift. What we receive from prayer, in fact, is the capacity to give more.

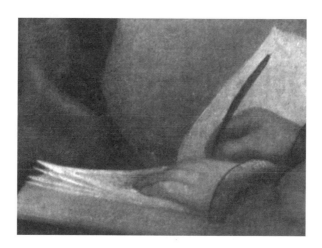

6

DIFFERENT VANTAGE
POINTS

In human relationships we are often surprised to encounter someone familiar to us in one situation operating in a completely different way in another. Men and women can seem quite different persons at home and at work. Our knowledge of a person may be quite defective if it is restricted to one type of situation. One of the best ways to deepen a friendship is to make a journey together. In a variety of unguarded situations each sees how the other reacts, new lights and shades are perceived, and the relationship must be continually redefined to cope with new complexities. The relationship becomes more real and comprehensive – with power to draw from the partners richer and more satisfying responses.

I imagine it must be similar in a marriage. In making life's journey together, husband and wife find new events throwing the familiar into unexpected relief, and revealing other facets of their complex personalities. The youthfulness evident in their wedding photographs is left behind; maturity comes, then middle age and beyond. There are places visited together and common friends. There are memories of joys and tragedies, of sleepless nights and brooding silences. And children who reflect, in a baffling way, the contradictory sum of parental qualities – and call forth new responses in both parties. If love grows stronger with the years this is not because it was defective at the start. It is because new situations evoke new qualities and provide added reasons for new love.

Our relationship with God is no more static than this. God may be unchanging – though it depresses me to think so. Certainly I am not. Our relationship has to accommodate itself to my changeable nature. And prayer, which reflects the relationship, is also subject to change. This is important. Saint John Cassian speaks about it in this way:

> I believe that it is impossible to grasp all the different forms of prayer without great purity of heart and soul. There are as many forms of prayer as there are states of soul or, rather, there are as many as the totality of states experienced by all souls together. We

are not able to perceive all the various kinds of prayer due to our inner debility, nevertheless, let us try to go through those which we know from our own far from extraordinary experience.

Prayer is fashioned anew from moment to moment according to the measure in which the mind is purified and according to the sort of situation in which it finds itself, whether this be the result of external contingencies or its own accomplishment. It is certain, moreover, that nobody is ever able to keep praying in the same way. A person prays in a certain manner when cheerful and in another when weighed down by sadness or a sense of hopelessness. When one is flourishing spiritually, prayer is different from when one is oppressed by the extent of one's struggles. One prays in this manner when seeking pardon for sins, and in another when asking for some grace or virtue or the elimination of a particular vice. Sometimes prayer is conditioned by compunction, occasioned by the thought of hell and the fear of judgement; at other times it is aflame with hope and desire for the good things to come. A person prays in one manner when in dangerous straits and in another when enjoying quiet and security. Prayer is sometimes illumined by the revelation of heavenly mysteries but, at other times, one is forced to be content with the sterile practice of virtue and the experience of aridity.[1]

In Cassian's mind two factors are responsible for change in prayer. One is spiritual growth – the degree to which the spirit is purified. The other is the impact of external circumstances. Each of these deserves comment.

It is not always stressed enough that prayer and religion develop together in the individual. Many people, for example, receive an intense and detailed religious formation during childhood. Come adulthood, ideally childhood faith has broken out of its husk and has re-formed in an adult mode. More than likely this has not happened. Sometimes religion is sloughed off, left behind as inappropriate to one's adult years. So it is, or at least childhood religion is. Sometimes religion becomes a symbol of something else – the Establishment or the previous generation – and is rejected. And sometimes it is left aside with a somber, if unspoken, sense of guilt – as being unable to include the specific deviancies of the individual. And sometimes religion is maintained, but as a childish form dressed in adult garb, unable to cope with major challenges should they arise. In so many cases individuals have rejected religion because they felt rejected by it.

By growing up they felt themselves excluded – like Adam and Eve from the garden of paradise.

As adults we need to think of religion in very inclusive terms, so as to reckon with the whole spectrum of human variation. Formation given in childhood is intended as a springboard for future evolution, whose details will be different for each individual. As the direction of one's life becomes more apparent with each personal choice, one's religion and one's prayer should adapt. If they do not, trouble is in store.

Prayer is too subtle a reality to be stereotyped. To build a definition of prayer on a narrow base is erroneous, and likely to be unjust. What is important is not judging the status of another's prayer but ensuring that our own prayer is authentic and that it corresponds to our state of growth, human and spiritual.

Prayer also varies according to external contingencies. Cassian includes both outer necessities – the demands of illness, hospitality, work, family and relaxation, for example – and things we undertake on our own initiative, that could have been avoided. We should build our prayer on a foundation of reality and not waste time on regrets. Take the situation, messy though it is, and begin from there. Whatever changes me changes my relationship with God: attempts at prayer must reflect this variation.

There is no real problem when prayer occurs spontaneously. It reaches out to us wherever we are, attracts our attention and draws us toward God. These unprogrammed moments draw their power from where we are. They are a natural bridge between one's actual situation and the unseen God. They vary because they are not in our control.

It is somewhat different with prayer practiced on a more regular basis. Because many things that disturb us during prayer have their basis in unrest, it is useful to learn techniques for stilling this disquiet. There is a danger that we may become satisfied with the self-oriented components of meditation – a sense of peace, togetherness and relief from anxiety – without adverting to the more important relational aspects. To concentrate too much on our own physical or psychological well-being is to stop short of the mark. Sometimes it may be better to flounder around, floating in and out of prayer, uncontrolled, so long as this gives us a sense of our need for God. This may be preferable to passing quickly into an advanced meditational state and staying there for a long period imbibing the nectar. Both experiences can be helpful; neither is intrinsically better. The more authentic is the one that more accurately reflects the truth of where I stand and makes me want God more.

Sometimes prayer seems to go well. The danger is that next time I come to pray, I try to re-create that prayer instead of trying to pray from where I am. In other words, I spend my time searching for yesterday's prayer. It has vanished as certainly as a champagne bubble. I cannot evade the task before me: I must pray from where I am today.

While pursuing life's journey we pray in many different ways, sometimes very deeply, sometimes shallowly. Dom John Chapman's maxim was "Pray as you can. Don't pray as you can't."[2] In the process I begin to see different facets of God; and mirroring God, I come to appreciate different facets of myself. The further we advance together on this journey, or rather the further I advance with and in and toward God, the more I am established in the truth about myself. It is hard to know which comes first, self-knowledge or an appreciation of the richness of God, but it is certainly true that they are closely associated. Once again, *The Cloud of Unknowing*:

> And so you must toil and sweat as much as you can to get a true knowing and feeling of yourself, a wretch as you are. Then, I believe, you will soon have a true knowing and feeling of God as he is ... as he wills to be known and experienced by a humble soul living in this mortal body.[3]

Self-knowledge and God-knowledge go hand in hand. In our progressive self-discovery we find in ourselves new beliefs about God. And we dare to face the unknown in ourselves only because we are intuitively aware that it resonates with something in God: for whatever is, to the extent that it is, derives its being from the Creator.

We have now reached a point in discussion of prayer where it is necessary to introduce a new element. Up to this, prayer has been presented as an *introspective* reality. Its inward character has been emphasized, its formlessness, and its lack of continuity with ordinary consciousness. The time has come to say something about ways prayer can be fed from outside – without, however, losing anything of its interiority.

Because we are social beings, the knowledge we have of God and of ourselves is not totally our private preserve. It is knowledge largely shared with other human beings. From them we can learn much of God and of ourselves. We are not so very different, after all.

Much in others' experience resonates in me. When I hear another's story a frequent first impulse is to think, "I have been there too," although at the level of fact that is not true. As an ancient poet remarked, "I am a human being and nothing that is human is alien to me." No human experience of good and evil is beyond me. I am no different in nature from anyone else.

Others teach me about a reality wider than my immediate experience. They also reveal to me something of my own inner qualities. In decision-making I am influenced, above all, by those who embody qualities I would willingly call mine.

A new element is introduced by the incarnation of the Word of God. God's Son embraces our nature without yielding anything of his divinity. In entering space and time and participating in our history, Christ demonstrated the total compatibility of the human and the divine. He has taken to the limit human potential for the divine. Only in the incarnate Word can we grasp the extent of our capacity for God.

The incarnation provides the pattern for our prayer. Whatever we learn about the person of Jesus Christ instructs us both in self-knowledge and in God-knowledge. Saint Augustine's saying became axiomatic in the centuries after: "Whatever Christ had by nature, we have by grace." Or as we find it expressed in the prologue of the fourth Gospel, "Of his fullness have we all received, grace for grace" (John 1:16).

Prayer, then, is a matter of our participating in the life of Jesus Christ. In him we have access to God's revelation of himself … and of us. The whole history of God's dealings with humankind, brought to a head in Christ becomes relevant to us (Ephesians 1:10). So also does the inspired record of those dealings.

Through the Scriptures we can traverse the centuries, experiencing the action of God vicariously, but really, from different vantage points. While we walk up and down the land of promise with Abraham (Genesis 13:17), we also explore our inner terrain. At least since Origen in the third century, there has been a conviction in the church that the events of salvation history as narrated in the Bible parallel the inner happenings of the soul's journey towards God. Many scriptural commentaries by the Fathers of the Church pursued this line of interpretation. The Scriptures are our tribal myths. They provide us with a framework for comprehending God's action in our lives, and motivate us to submit to it. While reading the Scriptures it is important to be aware of their inner resonances. Saint Athanasius, writing about the Psalms, says they can serve as a mirror for what is going on in our own souls.[4] There is no conflict between the inner and outer worlds; each complements and assists the other.

There is variation in our prayer because we look toward God from different vantage points. Our situation changes; we develop and are subjected to a range of external factors. Our situation can also change because we deliberately choose to seek further into the mystery of God. Having penetrated as far as we can (or dare) into our own hearts, we need to broaden the agenda and look searchingly into God's self-revelation. As we pass deeper into it we will find, to our surprise, that we are also penetrating more profoundly the mysterious space within.

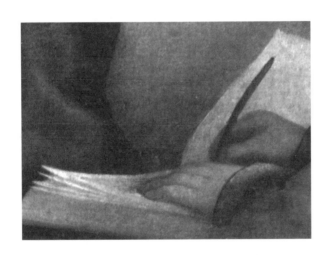

7

PONDERING
THE WORD

Among many people who wish to give themselves more fully to prayer there is a strong interest in techniques. Convinced of the importance of prayer, they are a little impatient of anything that smacks of being too theoretical. The practical question is, *How* do I pray or meditate or reach contemplation? Many answers are offered, and nearly all of them can take us some distance. The important thing is not to erect a few commonsense practical suggestions into a system that protects us from the insecurity necessary if we are to grow beyond the bounds of our own self-conceptions. Because prayer involves transcending self, we can never be quite in control.

Interest in techniques is not new. The author in *The Cloud of Unknowing* speaks of ways to prevent thoughts of sin from disturbing our prayer:

> And if [thoughts] rise often, as often put them down. To speak briefly, put them down as often as they rise. If you think that the travail is great, you may seek tricks and wiles and the secret subtleties of spiritual techniques to put these thoughts aside. Such devices are better learned from God by experience than from any human being in this life.[1]

It is legitimate to develop skills and acquire familiarity with practices that can help us maintain our wholeheartedness during prayer. But this, under God, is a task best undertaken by experiment. No means is better than another unless it serves to further our prayer. Still, we can learn from others, provided that we do not simply absorb their methods without discrimination. *The Cloud* continues in the next chapter: "Nevertheless, some of this subtlety shall I tell you, as it seems to me. Try it and do better if you can."[2]

Reading the Scriptures is often included among helps for prayer. This is specially so in schools of meditation that emphasize filling one's mind during prayer. They suggest that we quarry thoughts from the Scriptures on which to reflect, or images that may move us, or scenarios from the life of Christ in which we participate imaginatively. We read the text, absorb from it what we need, and then begin our meditation. Thus reading the Bible is a step in the direction of prayer.

A different way of using the Scriptures is the practice known as *lectio divina*, or holy reading. This has developed in Western monasticism for more than fifteen hundred years. Such holy reading is not preparation for prayer but prayer itself. It may be described as a technique of prayer. Its most salient characteristic is immense reverence for the Word.

We begin by re-animating our faith in the power the Word possesses to reach out to us wherever we are, and to provide the direction and zest we need to intensify our journey toward God.

> For the Word of God is living and full of energy; it cuts more effectively than any double-edged sword and it penetrates all the way through to the boundary of soul and spirit, joints and marrow. It makes a judgement on the desires and thoughts of the heart. There is no creature that goes unseen by it, for all are naked and uncovered to the eyes of the one to whom we must render an account (Hebrews 4:12–13).

The only appropriate attitude in taking up the Word of God is one of deep seriousness and submission. We do not seek to control or manipulate the Word, but allow it the freedom of our minds and hearts. We come as disciples for whom it is more fitting to be silent than to speak. There are times for sorting out thoughts, speaking about problems and putting into words what we feel toward God; there is also a time to be still, to wait, to listen. God's Word invites a listening with the "ears of the heart" to the Word that has power to save our souls (see James 1:21).

We may begin our holy reading with an appropriate short prayer: "Speak, Lord, for your servant is listening" (1 Samuel 2:10); "You have the words of everlasting life" (John 6:68), or "Lord, that I may see" (Luke 18:41). We may adopt the words that Mary, the mother of Jesus, addressed to the angelic messenger, "Behold the servant of the Lord; be it done to me according to your word" (Luke 1:38). In Psalm 119 we find many individual verses expressing the reverent expectancy with which one should approach God's Word.

This attitude is fundamental to the practice of *lectio divina*. It surrounds every aspect of the exercise. The reason is that we are moving into the presence of mystery. An observer might think I am simply reading a book. He may even guess from my external disposition that this is a special sort of reading, but then again he may not. If I am giving myself to this holy reading in the right spirit, the text being read becomes a window on deep mysteries within. I become aware of the truth about myself at this moment; and as I move around within that awareness, my being related to God, and drawn toward God, becomes less intangible. The reading may stop for a time, its purpose achieved. The soul is being nourished inwardly. This is no gimmick, no trick of thought or imagination, but faith-filled penetration into truth.

Sometimes a poet writes about a simple, external event in a way that moves a reader intensely. In relatively few words the poem condenses strong passion. I would not be so touched unless the poet had felt deeply on the occasion of writing. My feelings move in parallel with the poet's. The language of poetry is always dense: while describing some accessible event it intimates something deeper. Its artistry helps me discover something within myself; and the emotion is stronger for my being surprised by it. The poem touches me; I am passive before it. It has power to release latent feeling.

The Scriptures are largely written, if not in poetry, certainly in a mysterious language of similitude and parable. They are more than a disinterested record of events in a distant world long ago. They are documents of faith: "These things are written so that you might believe" (John 20:31). The historical memories selected are precisely those that have a certain transparency, allowing the reader to recognize a general pattern with the specific instance, a pattern that operates still. "All these things which happened to them occurred as a symbol and they were written down as a warning for us" (1 Corinthians 10:11).

We need to begin reading convinced that a deep affinity already exists between us and what we are about to read. The Word is not only external; it is implanted in our hearts (James 1:21). There is no question here of being brainwashed or overwhelmed by an external body of doctrine – rather of seeds already sown and ready to grow. (Mark 4:14). By attending to the Word we are tending the growth of our spiritual life. And the God who speaks through the Scriptures is already known to us because he dwells within.

Several practical consequences flow from the requirement of reverence. In general, since holy reading is prayer, anything that helps us into prayer will help with *lectio divina*. The more general helps will be discussed in a later chapter. Here a few specific points are offered.

What is holy is our *reading* of the text, that is, welcoming it into a believing heart. The text itself possesses a sacredness too. No harm will be done by surrounding the book of the Bible with care and love. It helps to have as good an edition as our budget allows. We should respect and cherish our Bible, not scribbling on it – as if to impose our own poor thoughts upon the text – but reverencing it in its integrity. A Bible that is familiar and has become a prayer companion can itself help lead us into an atmosphere of quiet and receptivity.

Second, one needs to be convinced that the text of the Bible being used is substantially accurate. There are a number of modern, critical translations. An edition with notes helps some readers to reach more deeply into the meaning of the text. For many the quality of the language is also important, although tastes differ here. Some language facilitates the process of depthing by virtue of the associations it creates or, perhaps, by avoiding the connotations of everyday parlance.

Third, our reverence for the Word of God should create a sincere effort of attention. Saint Caesarius of Arles makes this clear in one of his sermons:

> Brothers and sisters, here is a question for you; Which to you seems the greater, the Word of God or the Body of Christ? If you want to give the right answer, you will reply that God's Word is not less than Christ's Body. Therefore, just as we take care when we receive the Body of Christ so that no part of it falls to the ground, so should we likewise ensure that the Word of God which is given to us is not lost to our souls because we are speaking or thinking about something different. One who listens negligently to God's Word is just as guilty as one who, through carelessness, allows Christ's Body to fall to the ground.[3]

There needs to be some effort to ensure that our mind is uncluttered before we begin holy reading. Then we can give ourselves with some serenity to listening and to receiving. Some interruptions are inevitable – but others we seem to invite. To make reading an occasion of deeper prayer, one must concentrate on the text and not slip away.

Fourth, we come to *lectio divina* without an agenda, not mapping out in advance what we hope to experience or receive. Like all prayer, holy reading is an exercise in dedication. We come to allow God to act upon us. This means not seeking prescriptions for our ills. We accept what comes, whether consolation or challenge. Many people look to the Bible for comfort and are dismayed when they do not receive it. It is a sober fact that God frequently withholds relief, to correct our vices and render our hearts more responsive. As Saint Augustine explains:

> To the extent that the Word of God is going to help in the correction of our lives, in causing you to hope for reward and to fear punishment, all must make a judgement about themselves in all honesty and not to try and find comfort when really they are placed in a dangerous situation. You notice that the Lord God does not offer such comfort. It is true that he does console us by promising good things and by strengthening our hope. But for those of evil life, those who spurn his Word, there is no relief. Therefore, let all of us ask ourselves, while there is still time, whether we are persevering in doing good and turning away from the doing of evil.[4]

God's Word leads to greater truth; for us to try controlling the process means that we remain fixed in our own sphere of half-truth and delusion.

Fifth (a consequence of the last point), reverence for the whole message of the Scriptures should make us reluctant to treat the Bible as a lucky dip from which oracles may be extracted at random. The Scriptures do not work by magic; they were composed to be read by intelligent beings. To look for a text which expresses a particular sentiment is to empty the Scriptures of their power. And taking any text at random seems to deny the Bible its own contextual meaning. I remember once being with a group who approached the Scriptures in random fashion. The text selection began with John 8:44, "You come from your father who is the devil, and your will is to fulfil the desires of your father ... Those who are of God listen to the words of God; you do not listen, therefore you are not of God." And much more of the same. As if to confirm that those present were not listening to the Word of God, the reader continued and continued until she arrived at a "nice" passage. The whole exercise seemed to suggest that any nasty or unpredictable saying is to be ignored. The challenge was smothered in cotton wool.

Respecting the literary integrity of the Bible means that, in general, we think in terms of books, rather than flitting about reading a chapter here and there. Take the letters of Saint Paul. In their present form, they are constructed as units. Paul first makes friends with his readers, then offers a doctrinal section, and finally gets down to business with concrete recommendations about practical, everyday conduct. To confine oneself to the greetings and thanksgivings may convert one's reading into an exercise in self-congratulation. We need to broaden our theological vision and to begin to think practically about how our new insights can be embodied in behavior. There is a unity here: doctrine supports moral teaching. Without moral corollaries, theology becomes unreal.

I suggest, then, that we base our *lectio divina* on books of the Bible rather than on individual chapters, incidents or texts. Because such reading is slow, we may need several months to work through a book. Quantity is not important; the consistency and integrity of our reading are. A profound book such as Jeremiah could easily extend over the better part of a year. On each occasion we return, seeking God's will – and seeing it somewhat differently as the new text shines through the prism of our own changing experience.

Before praying a book of the Bible, it may help to peruse it rapidly with the aid of a good commentary – to become aware of its structure and characteristics, and get a feeling for its specific approach. Later, we may be less disturbed by questions while praying the text through. If something interests us during holy reading, note it and pursue the matter at another time. In general, it is good to dispose of as many potential distractions as possible before approaching the book in prayer. Many resources are readily available. Consulting them is not mere scholarship. It comes from a concern to understand as accurately as possible the revelation God has implanted in fragile human words.

Sixth, our reverence for the Word of God will lead us toward obedience. It is not enough to receive the Word, one must have the antecedent willingness to put it into practice. So I come into the presence of the Word knowing full well that my life may be changed, and in a way that is not of my constructing. I come to the Word consenting to hear the call and praying for strength to respond affirmatively. I come prepared to wait, knowing that only in the long term do real results become apparent.

If entered with heartfelt reverence, our reading of the Scriptures becomes a deep experience and merits being seen as prayer. Our reading will be holy, and most incidental problems encountered in its practice will quickly slip away.

I offer three further practical suggestions. The first concerns our choice of reading. I have already proposed reading books as a whole, as a general rule. If we find ourselves attracted to an isolated passage, it is good to remain there as long as the attraction lasts. But normally it is worthwhile staying with a book, working through it from beginning to end. It pays then to be reasonably careful in making the initial choice. Those who try to spend a long time reading Leviticus may find their patience tried beyond endurance. We may choose to follow some sort of system – working serially through the major books, or alternating Old and New Testaments, or changing from one type of book to another. Some may prefer to follow their own intuition: "I think I will read Isaiah" – or the Letter to the Hebrews, or whatever. In one sense it scarcely matters since it is the same God whom we meet throughout the Scriptures; varying the approach means that we come to see God from different angles.

So far, I have restricted the scope of *lectio divina* to the Scriptures. Can other books qualify? The short answer is yes, so long as they induce in us the same response of reverent passivity, so that the critical faculties may be temporarily unemployed. This present book does *not* qualify. The Scriptures are guaranteed as inspired. My inspiration is strictly limited. Books that can be read as *lectio divina* are generally those recognized as expressing the faith of the Church, rather than the occasional reflections of an individual. Thus liturgical texts qualify, as do the official teachings of the Church – although some of these are couched in a language little suited to devotion. I myself devote much time to the Fathers of the Church. This experience is different from reading the Bible, but is still holy reading; it remains more like prayer than study. For me the two sources of reading are complementary. They feed into each other and are mutually enriching. For those with the time and opportunity to include the Fathers of the Church in their reading, I would strongly recommend such a step. But this is neither possible nor advisable for everyone. The same principles hold for reading other Doctors of the Church; if they speak to us with authority so that we can find in their writings the faith of the Church, they could well become part of our diet of holy reading.

A person praying regularly may soon feel a need to read more widely about the dynamics of spirituality. While this is good and worthwhile, our supporting reading must remain secondary; it should not be allowed to encroach on our *lectio divina*, nor become a substitute for prayer.

My next suggestion may at first seem a little bizarre. I strongly recommend reading aloud or, if this is not possible, vocalizing the text as one reads it. This was the ancient way of reading, long before the advent of speed reading, and it still serves a number of useful purposes.

- Vocalizing the text slows us down; it does not permit one's eyes to race over the page, but causes one to go steadily, dwelling on each phrase – not merely to extract its obvious meaning, but to reach deeper down into its depths and into one's own.

- A vocalized text has more impact on us. In the liturgy, a text makes far more impression on us when we are acting as readers than when we are passive recipients. Not only its meaning, but also its poetry, seem more potent when we are actively involved in its proclamation.

- Vocalizing the text is a good means of avoiding distractions. It is almost physically impossible to read a text aloud and allow the mind to wander somewhere else. The words begin to be jumbled, and we are alerted. So vocalization serves to focus the mind's energies and give them direction.

- Presuming that we do not normally read in this way, vocalization makes our *lectio divina* a distinctive exercise, and operates as a reminder when our resolution wavers. We slip away often from the full intensity of prayer, and need something to keep coming back to. Renewing our outward reading of the text is one way of confirming our willingness of heart.

- Vocalization is also an aid to memory. A text spoken and heard remains more firmly imprinted in the memory than one merely seen. (The role of memory in extending our prayer throughout the day is discussed in the next chapter.)

In the Middle Ages, the word *meditatio* was not restricted to mental activity. It was viewed instead as musing, an almost audible process of repeating texts to oneself, a rumination. It was certainly not a high-powered operation, like a quick raid into a text to grab the meaning and make an escape. More like a friendship, a cherishing, whereby one lived with a text that had become particularly dear, exploring it from different vantage points, saying it to oneself in a quiet, non-analytic way and letting it act on the heart. This process reached throughout the day and into every corner of life. Its beginning was in the practice of holy reading.

One final practical suggestion: if *lectio divina* is to be a technique of prayer and not mere reading, it is helpful to surround it by prayer. Sometimes the prayer inherent in a text has to be primed. We may begin with a short prayer, expressing our dependence on God for any help we might receive, and in a special way calling on the aid of the Holy Spirit. If reading leaves us prayerless, we may insert prayer. If the text continues to be dry for us, we might cautiously increase the speed a little. Alternatively, it might be better to stop and ask, "Why am I unable to pray today?" Often the problem is not in the text but in ourselves, and it is necessary to explore the roots of our restlessness. Today's may not be the kind of prayer we anticipated. Now, through our own inability to cope with the text, we have been led in prayer to confront our real situation.

Our reading often acts as a kind of spiritual barometer, revealing through the medium of our reactions where we stand at a given time. Sometimes reading helps uncover our spiritual sensitivities, and may even release prayer we did not know was in us. At other times it may expose our desperate need for salvation and lead into a different kind of prayer, a humble appeal to God to be delivered from difficulties. One thing is certain; the prayer of *lectio divina*, like other modes of prayer, leads to a life progressively more oriented toward God. The particular value of holy reading is that it supplies incentives to prayer from outside – and keeps us from the fatal error of self-programming.

Like Mary, mother of the Lord, "who kept all these words, pondering them in her heart" (Luke 2:19), we are called to welcome our God with all possible openness. In holy reading we do this initially through contact with the Scriptures. Even at that stage, prayer is powerfully present. But it becomes even more evident as the cumulative effect of *lectio divina* practised over a long period. Fidelity to God's Word leaves a residue in the mind that generates further prayer spontaneously – even in wildly unfavorable circumstances. This development is traced in the chapters that follow.

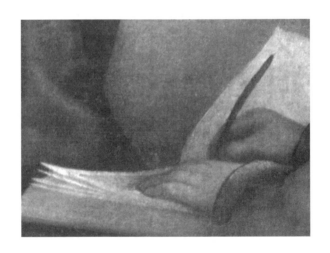

8

MODELS OF PRAYER

There is an element of "delayed reaction" in holy reading that varies from person to person. Some find the practice of *lectio divina* sufficient to evoke the prayer within them. They are drawn easily into reflection and this gives birth to prayer of increasing depth. For others, most of the action takes place after they close the book. As they perform daily tasks, thoughts surface that make them turn toward God. Many, like myself, experience both dynamics.

I want now to discuss further what happens after we rise from our reading. William of St Thierry suggests we always try to take away some morsel to nibble on through the day – something that speaks to our situation at the time, and may help us assess life's circumstances in the light of God's Word. Here is his text:

> Some part of your daily reading should, each day, be stored in the stomach, that is in the memory, so that it may be digested. At times it should be brought up again for frequent rumination. You should select something that is in keeping with your calling and in line with your personal orientation, something which will seize hold of your mind and not allow it to think over alien matters.[1]

God's Word frequently yields its meaning only slowly, as we attempt to explore its depths and translate it into behavior. In the attempting and the failing we really begin to hear God's message. Cumulatively, *lectio divina* bears fruit in the renewal of our lives.

It is helpful to do something definite to build a bridge between holy reading and the rest of one's life. The most common device is to commit part of what we read to paper. If something strikes us as having particular relevance or significance now, we should quietly write it down – not scribble it on a scrap of old paper like a telephone message to be acted on and then thrown out. It should be given a nobler format, written on a card or in a book so that the very act of writing is a meditative gesture, another way of taking to heart what the text is saying. Some people find it helpful to keep a kind of journal where they record texts that speak powerfully to them. If this is done with care, the journal can be used years later to recapture moments of grace. This was a common practice in the monasteries of the Middle Ages, where monks, according to the availability of writing materials, constructed *catenae* (chains) or *florilegia* (bouquets) of scriptural texts. These threw light on a particular subject by drawing on many years of quiet reading and meditation.

Some people get to the heart of a text by "dialoguing" with what they have written – or with the Lord, or even with themselves. Of one or other they ask, "What do you want of me? How can I hear what you are saying and allow it to shape my life?" Yet another response is to write a short prayer or "collect" based on what we have read. If one really listens to the Word one becomes acutely aware of one's own needs and those of the whole human family. Our reading can then be summarized in a prayer that recalls what God has revealed and prays that the desires one has received will find fulfillment. These are simple techniques that can be helpful so long as we do not become enslaved to them.

Paper and cards are one thing: the memory is better. Although not much cultivated or esteemed today, the memory can be useful in our search for prayer. If, as Solzhenitsyn suggests, forgetfulness of God is the principal cause of all human woes, then remembering God becomes a significant step on the path to recovery.[2] And if evil thoughts are the beginning of moral decline, thoughts of God, as in the case of the Prodigal Son, indicate the way back (Luke 15:17–18).

Saint Basil took up this point in one of his collections of rules for monastic living:

> Therefore we ought to keep our heart with all watchfulness lest the desire for God be dislodged and driven from our souls by evil desires and filthy thoughts. On the contrary, let each one of us set on our souls the seal of the divine form and figure by means of the assiduous recollection and memory of God. Then that seal will not be moved by any disturbances whatever. If the fire of desire for divine charity burns in us, then the mind and the soul will be illuminated by the frequent memory of God and we will be lifted up and raised for the task of keeping his commandments.[3]

To live in accord with the Gospel, we must bear its message in mind and heart – that is, live in mindfulness.

I am not saying that we should learn by rote large segments of the Scriptures. But there is no harm in becoming so familiar with significant texts that they begin to appear in our awareness quite unexpectedly. A small card with a text on it may help at first, but progressively we have the text "by heart." Then, when we want to pray, but do not know how to get started, the text we have internalized can help. Sometimes it is only a matter of getting the wheels turning, finding a way of access to the depths beneath our daily business.

The Bible is, in fact, a great quarry of prayer. In its pages there is prayer for almost every conceivable situation. Some people easily gauge where they are at any given moment, and find no difficulty in translating that awareness to prayer. This is not always possible. Sometimes a text can help. Using a text in prayer is like sending a greeting card. The words are not less sincere because they are not original. Sometimes our need to express love goes beyond our ability with words.

It need not be artificial or impersonal to use existing forms of address to God in prayer. Many of the texts that have come down to us, sifted through the centuries, express in a powerful way emotions we all feel at some stage of our journey toward God. In fact sometimes we can express ourselves with greater personal intensity, because these models relieve us of the tension of creativity.

Jesus Christ gave us the Our Father as a typical prayer (Matthew 6:9–13; Luke 11:2–4). Similarly, in his own prayer in the garden of Gethsemane, he has given us the example of an impassioned plea for deliverance, mysteriously mingled with submission (Mark 14:36). In reading the Gospels we come across many prayers we can spontaneously make our own as we read: "Give us always this bread" (John 6:34), "Lord, save me" (Matthew 14:30), "I do believe, help my unbelief" (Mark 9:24). It seems the evangelists have deliberately patterned their accounts to include these invitations to the reader to participate in the action. The Psalms belong with a number of other poetic compositions scattered through the two Testaments. There is great value in making friends with such texts, since they can carry our prayer through periods when other ways of praying bring only chagrin.

The Psalms express a range of emotion that far exceeds our

normal powers of language. Some of them express sentiments that we would not otherwise dare expose to ourselves or to others – and ones we would certainly try to shield from God. By expressing these feelings before God, we face up to them. In confronting our own discontent, we are already close to genuine prayer, and certainly in a better state psychologically than if we tried to bottle up our unhappiness and use religion as the stopper.

We are also likely to repress sentiments of joy and thankfulness. For those especially who feel oppressed by hardships, life can easily pass without its moments of truth and beauty being sufficiently celebrated. These aspects of life are forgotten – not denied, just overlooked. It is good to recognize that while human existence can seem half-empty, it is in fact *at least* half-full.

It may be helpful to look in detail at some models of prayer in the Scriptures. They have much to teach and can lead us into prayer with a minimum of fuss. Let us begin with Psalm 123:

> To you who dwell in the heavens
> have I lifted up my eyes.
> As the eyes of a servant
> are on the hands of his master,
> as the eyes of a handmaid
> are on the hands of her mistress,
> so are our eyes on the Lord our God,
> waiting for his mercy.
> Have mercy, O Lord, have mercy
> for we are full of much contempt.
> Our very soul is full of much contempt,
> scorned by the rich,
> despised by the proud.

Alongside great sensitivity to suffering, there is great serenity here. Pain is not put aside but embraced, absorbed – not lessened, but gently brought into a wider vision. From the midst of affliction the psalmist raises his eyes to God in a universal gesture of hope and expectancy. There is no clamor here, just great humility. Like an attentive servant, the author waits in trust and confidence for a gesture signalling that the prayer has been heard. I cannot think of a better school of prayer than this psalm. Yet because prayer is potentially such a rich reality, there are scores of other texts to lead us equally effectively into some awareness of our relationship with God, bringing to the fore different aspects of that relationship.

Those who have tasted the cup of bitterness need not feel there is any part of their experience that cannot be brought before the Lord in all its intensity. They may come to identify with every verse of Psalm 88, or with certain passages from the book of Job, or with the canticle of Hezekiah in Isaiah 38. They may need to pray from the extremity of their anguish – with all its self-contradictory features – in words such as those in Jeremiah 20:7–18.

> You enticed me, O Lord, and I was enticed
> for you were stronger than I
>   and you have prevailed.
> Now have I become all day long
>   an object of derision;
> everyone mocks me.
> Whenever I utter the Word, I bellow aloud
>   and what I call out is "Violence and disaster!"
> For me the word of the Lord has been
>   a source of scorn
>   and abuse all day long.
> So I said to myself,
>   "I will no longer be mindful of it.
>   I will not speak any more in his name."
> Then there was within my heart,
>   as it were, an outburst of flame.
>   It was shut within my bones.
> I exhausted myself trying to restrain it,
>   and I was not able.
> For I hear many saying, "Terror from every side."
>   "Denounce him! Let us denounce him!"
> All those who used to wish me well
>   have become watchers for my stumbling:
>   "Perhaps he will be led astray and make a mistake;
>   then we will take him and wreak vengeance upon him."
> But the Lord is with me as an awe-inspiring warrior,
> so that those who persecute me will slip,
>   they shall not prevail.
> They will be greatly put to shame and come to nothing,
> an everlasting reproach which will not be forgotten.
> O Lord Sabaoth, righteous examiner,
> who penetrate feeling and thought,

let me see you take revenge on them,
for it is to you that I have entrusted my cause.
   O sing to the Lord!
   Praise the Lord!
   For he has delivered the life of the needy
   from the hand of the wicked.
Cursed be the day on which I was born,
the day my mother gave me birth!
Cursed be the man who brought news to my father:
   "A son is born to you – a male!"
   thus making him happy.
Let that man be like the cities
   which the Lord ruthlessly destroyed!
In the morning, let him hear a cry of alarm
   and, at midday, the shout of battle.
For he did not kill me in the womb
   so that my mother would have been my grave,
   her womb forever pregnant.
Why did I ever leave the womb
   to see only toil and sorrow,
   to end my days in shame?

Few more strongly worded complaints to God exist. This is no text to use every day. But it is consoling to know that if our sufferings ever reach the extreme of Jeremiah's, we can still appear before God without dissimulating our true feelings. What is significant here is that within the overwhelming gloom there are glimmers of hope: Jeremiah is aware that his vocation comes from God – and that the rejection he experiences is directed less at him than at God's message. He attests the strength of God that overcame his reluctance to serve, and sees a brief flash of hope as he glimpses God's ultimate victory. The same ambiguity can occur in our own anguish; confronting the worst we find, it ceases to exercise tyranny over us.

There is a sense in which the very act of addressing such a complaint to God is the beginning of its solution. What we fear above all is the unnameable. Being able to speak of a terror relativizes it. The possibility of reaching out to God from the depths of our affliction indicates that a bit of our faith survives. The cry of Jesus on the cross, "My God, My God, why have you forsaken me?" (Mark 15:34), stemmed from a sense of deep abandonment. Yet the cry itself was a rising from those depths toward God. It was not a moment when Jesus retreated from his pain into himself, but a moment of intense reaching out toward the Father. And immediately Jesus was assumed into God. Even strong grief can bring a person to reach out beyond self into mystery. There is a sense in which the psalms of lamentation are always said in irony as if hinting that in spite of an excess of bitterness, there is still hope. This tension is intensified when such psalms are used in the liturgy, and are concluded with a doxology. They seem to say, "Behold my woes, yet still I give you thanks."

One finds a curious mingling of defeat and triumph, of petition and praise, of despair and thanksgiving, in many texts. This, too, is instructive: prayer is to reflect the duality of our experiences. Besides, a change often occurs during prayer: we can begin at one pole and gradually find our attention moving toward the other. We may begin with woe and end in praise. If we come to prayer in gratitude and joy, we may find our purest exaltation needs to be purified. If prayer is real, in no way is it a rubber stamp for our moods.

Sometimes, as in the canticle of Hezekiah already mentioned, it is difficult to decide whether a text is primarily thanksgiving or petition. The text is presented as the prayer made by the king *after* his recovery from the mortal illness; yet the opening section is so graphic and so dulled by pain that reading it for the first time one is overwhelmed by its hopelessness. Suddenly the lamentation gives way to joy. The poet has switched from an awareness of self to an awareness of God, and all is changed.

The same dynamic occurs in the song of thanksgiving that Jonah sang in the belly of the great fish. In the context of the book, the raging sea was the enemy. The whale (if whale it was) is presented as God's instrument for saving Jonah from the sea, which represents the forces of chaos unleashed by Jonah's refusal to render obedience.

> [And Jonah prayed to the Lord his God from inside the fish. And he said:]
>
> I called in my distress
>   to the Lord who answered me.
> From the womb of the underworld I cried for help:
>   you heard my cry.

You cast me into the depths,
    in the heart of the sea
and the currents carried me away.
All your billows and breakers
    passed over me.
And I said, "I am driven away
    from before your eyes.
How shall I ever see again
    your holy temple?"
The waters are about me, to my neck,
    the vast ocean surrounds me;
      reeds encircle my head.
In the extremities of the mountains
I descend to a world
    where bars enclose me forever.
From the pit you brought me up alive
    O Lord my God.
As my life deserted me
    I remembered the Lord.
My prayer went up to you
    in your holy temple.
Those who have a care for vanities
    forsake their loyalties.
But with the sound of praise shall I
    make sacrifice to you.
My vows I will render in full.
    Salvation is from the Lord! (Jonah 2:2–10)

Suffering and oppression open us out for the experience of deliverance. If we are fortunate, our sense of God as deliverer or savior strengthens and expands through the years. We find peace and joy in the awareness of God's love, and slowly the thought sinks in that this love is the ultimate source of all that is good. It gives rise to the beauty of the world around us, the accomplishments of others, the love of our friends and the love within. So an instinct develops to praise God whenever we encounter a reflection of his beauty. Psalm 104 does this magnificently, surveying the whole gamut of creaturely activity and seeing everywhere signs of the Creator's love, skill and playfulness. The more introspective Psalm 8 marvels that all this beauty and variety is at our service. Who must we be, then, if the whole exuberant creation pales in our presence?

O Lord, our God,
how far-reaching is your name:
it is present throughout the earth!
Your fame is celebrated in song
which rises above the heavens
from the mouths of babes and sucklings.
You have made for yourself a stronghold,
    because of your adversaries,
    to silence enemies and rebels.
I see the heavens, the work of your fingers,
the moon and the stars which you have made firm.
What is man that you have remembered him,
the son of Adam that he becomes your concern?
You have made him little less than the gods,
and crowned him with glory and splendour.
You have made him master over the works of your hand,
and put all things under his feet.
All flocks and herds
and the wild beasts as well;
the birds of the sky and the fish of the sea,
wending their way in the waters.
O Lord, our God,
how far-reaching is your name:
it is present throughout the earth!

The psalm models a contemplative stance before creation, seeing there a mirror of God's action and an invitation to celebrate God's work.

Whenever we give thanks and find joy in God's presence, we are not carefully singling out one particular aspect for praise. Our heart knows we are keeping jubilee for all God has done: in creation, in deliverance, in the gift of Jesus Christ, in all that has brought us to this point in life. We can therefore take a text like the Magnificat, which Saint Luke places on the lips of Mary, mother of the Lord, and pray with a vast, cosmic awareness of all God has done. On our own, we might have been tongue-tied in wonder; but we have been given words full of the Spirit who scans the depths of our hearts (Romans 8:27).

My soul magnifies the Lord,
my spirit is glad in God my savior.
He has looked on the lowliness of his handmaid

so that, from this time, all generations
   will call me the blessed one.
The mighty One, whose name is holy,
has accomplished great things for me.
For he has mercy on those who fear him,
from generation to generation.
His arm has been strong in action
scattering those who are haughty of heart.
He has deposed the powerful from their thrones,
the lowly has he elevated.
With good things he has filled the famished,
sending the rich away empty.
He has upheld his servant Israel,
mindful of his mercy.
As he spoke unto our fathers,
   to Abraham and to his descendants forever. (Luke 1:46–55)

This text suggests, in its Gospel context, that the gift of salvation may cause us to break out in song. Like many great figures of the Old Testament, Mary rejoices wholeheartedly about an intervention of God. Yet her jubilation and thanks mingle with a profound sense of unworthiness. Salvation is such a great gift no human achievement could merit it.

By using such texts of the Bible we can come to grips with those regions of our being that lie beyond thought. Some psalms and other texts we may care to learn by heart. Others may become familiar almost without our noticing. We glance at the page, and our lips seem to remember the rhythm of the words. Soon it is reciting itself, while we stand passively before it much moved – and turned toward God.

Fragments from the liturgy can be used in this way. It is worthwhile building up a small collection of liturgical prayers that attract us. We will often find that they express what we feel succinctly and profoundly. Hymns can serve the same purpose. I hasten to add that what is at issue here is no superficial practice of piety, but a question of ways in which deep movements of the heart can be allowed to rise and be reinforced. If we do not feel attracted to prayer, we should perhaps do no more than a minimum. Certainly there is no value in making life miserable by dosing ourselves with religion when no insistent demand is coming up from the depths.

By learning to love the Scriptures and to use them as prayer we ensure that our prayer is formed by God's inspired Word. We soon discover that a familiar text can be used to stir up prayer when it is sluggish, or help us with prayer in difficult times. Letting the Word of God flow freely in and out of the mind develops in us an aptitude for prayer that leads to a transformation of life. In time, many sins and deformities are eliminated and the person blossoms. To turn toward God is to become fully alive. We conclude then with Psalm 1:

> How great is the happiness of the man or woman
> who did not walk by the counsel of the wicked,
> who did not stand in the way of sinners
> nor sit in the assembly of the contemptuous.
> Such a one takes delight in the law of the Lord,
> pondering this law day and night;
> like a tree transplanted near streams of water
> yielding fruit in season,
> with leaves always green,
> prospering in all that is done.
> Not so are the wicked:
> they are like chaff which the wind blows away.
> The wicked shall not be left standing at the judgement
> and sinners shall not be included in the assembly of the
> righteous.
> For the Lord watches over the righteous,
> but the way of the wicked leads nowhere.

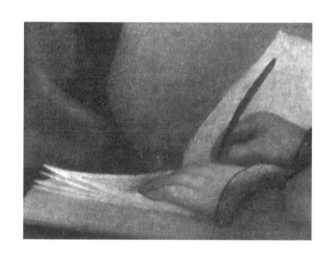

9

SHORT PRAYERS

Our Lord's warning against wordy prayer in the Sermon on the Mount (Matthew 6:7) was taken seriously by the Fathers of the Church. They saw dangers in speaking too much *(multiloquium)* during prayer, believing that chatter prevents communication going beyond superficiality. We have all experienced being prevented from passing on important news because the conversation never reached a suitable point. In hospital, for example, patients have time and solitude to reflect on matters that may not ordinarily occupy them much. Sometimes they would dearly love to speak about their insights, but their visitors supply so much cheerful banter that they dare not speak of what is in their hearts. It is easy to fill a void with trivia. Not doing so is a condition for reaching deeper and more personal levels of communication.

Speaking of prayer as conversation with God has the advantage of being instantly comprehensible. We may think of it as telephoning heaven. The disadvantage is that the mystery of prayer takes much more work than that to understand. True, there is psychological benefit in having imaginary conversations with God or the saints. This can help us clarify our own thoughts and feelings: often we discover within ourselves the answers to problems. This is pious and helpful, but there is much more to prayer. Perhaps the most comprehensible benefit of prayer for men and women today is the help it offers in moving to a deeper zone of humanity. Religion that parrots the preoccupations of ordinary consciousness is rightly seen as superfluous. No wonder sensitive persons of all ages feel estranged from this kind of practice. And prayer goes deeper than merely "processing" our lives. It is a search for God through seeking out our own hearts. It implies a quieting down on the conscious level so that what is going on beyond consciousness becomes more apparent.

Saint Cyprian insists on "sobriety" in prayer, lest our talkativeness swamp the subtle voice of the Spirit.[1] Saint Benedict belongs in the same tradition. Speaking of the need for quietness in the oratory, he says: "And if it happens that a brother wants to pray secretly, on his own, let him simply go in and pray, but not with a loud voice: rather with tears and the intent of his heart."[2] Elsewhere he repeats this idea: "We should know that we will be heard not for our much speaking but for our undividedness of heart and our compunction of tears."[3]

It makes sense then that we do not entirely identify our prayer with the words we use. A particular text of Scripture may arouse us spiritually so that prayer comes easily. What is important is the prayer evoked, not the text that serves to begin it. Once in a state of prayer, we may choose to leave aside the text, or stay with it only distantly. This is a natural development.

Everything depends on our desire to move toward God and on our willingness to seize opportunities as they open up. If there is some deep, inner block that makes me draw back, the process will not be carried any further until this is addressed. It is useless fiddling with prayer techniques in the hope of arriving at a workable combination. One's latent unwillingness to pursue some matters further has to be faced and defused before any advance is possible.

Words are important in prayer, but they must eventually become transparent. They are not the primary reality and cannot occupy the major part of my attention. I use words to get me started; often enough I stay with them, because in some odd way they relate to a wordless prayer in my heart. It is as though the words are a window onto my own depths, through which something of my inner reality peeps out. Sometimes my gaze is so intense that I cease to notice the window, and cannot rightly say whether the words are still there or not. The song is over, as it were, but the melody lingers on.

In our prayer, words tend to become richer by association, and so are needed less. What is important is that particular texts begin to assume great value for one's prayer; so even the smallest fragment may be enough to nourish prayer a long time.

I am not content with distinctions between "mental prayer" and "vocal prayer," especially when used to suggest that somehow "mental prayer" is higher and better than anything else. The only prayer with any value is one that rises from the heart in response to the realities of life. There is no theoretical scale on which the relative worth of prayers can be measured. Sometimes my prayer is a time of great inner stillness, and my spirit is possessed by what feels like God's nearness. That is good prayer. At other times I am tired and disgruntled; my efforts at prayer simply expose me to the specter of my own weakness, and I cry out to God from a very great distance. That also is good prayer. Prayer may be rejoicing in the Spirit or writhing in anguish; it is good if it is real, and no good if it is delusion or play-acting. As God's children we can feel free to use words or not. We do not need to worry much about the forms we use. God often makes possible a very intense prayer through means we regard as elementary. We are seeking a God who is above words and concepts. God is above them but we are not – and never will be in this life. So we have to be content with using words, as necessary, and leave the prospect of blissful spiritual communion mostly for the next life.

The kernel of prayer is desire – in the words of Saint Benedict quoted above, "intent of the heart." But this inward stretching forth of our being toward God is such a naked reality that the mind finds it hard to grasp. It can seem nebulous and without form. Words provide approximations to this mysterious reality and allow its influence to extend for a longer period. What would a relationship between two lovers be without expression in words – even though love is not fully expressed. Our desire for God is even less capable of being reduced to words; it is larger than life. Language is woefully inadequate to describe what transpires at the depths of our being. We cannot hope for an exact correlate of interior processes, but we *can* be helped by approximations, especially overlapping ones, that convey part of the truth.

This seems to be the mind of the author of *The Cloud of Unknowing* when he suggests encapsulating our prayer in a single word. This text is important and worth giving in full:

> Therefore, when you decide to undertake this work and feel by grace that you are called by God, lift up your heart to God with a meek stirring of love. Have God in mind who made you and redeemed you and who graciously calls you to this work. Accept no other thought of God, not even all of these, but only as you desire. A naked intent directed towards God is sufficient without any other cause but God.
>
> If you desire to have this intent enclosed in a word so that you can grasp it better, take a little word of one syllable. This is better than two syllables, because the shorter the word, the better it

SHORT PRAYERS   9 3

accords with the work of the Spirit. Such a word is "God" or "Love." Choose the one you prefer or some other, if you desire. Fasten this word to your heart so that it never departs whatever happens.

This word will be your shield and spear whether you ride in peace or war. With this word you shall beat on this cloud and this darkness above you. With this word you can smite all kinds of thoughts and place them under the cloud of forgetting. Thus, if any thought intrude and ask you what you want you can answer it with just this word alone. And if a thought offers, like a great scholar, to speak about your word and to explain it, reply that you want to have this word whole, not broken up and undone. And if you hold fast to this purpose, you can be certain that this distraction will cease.[4]

The key image here is of the "naked intent direct unto God" – the outreaching of the heart's desire, being somehow contained, "lapped and folden," in a single word chosen intuitively to serve this purpose. The author gives as examples "God" and "love;" elsewhere he adds "sin," "fire" and "out," each word embodying one of the moods of prayer. In his view we should gauge the atmosphere of the prayer within us, then select a short prayer or a word to encapsulate it.

The Cloud insists on a word of one syllable. This is often the practice in the East Asian use of a mantra. The sound of a single syllable can be prolonged to coincide with the breathing, and there is a certain sharpness about it that allows the mind no freedom to wander. Many people, however, find a single syllable a little stark, unfeeling or abrupt. They choose a longer word such as "Abba," "Jesus," "Amen" or "Alleluia," or may even prefer a short phrase such as "Marána, tha!" "Veni, Sancte Spiritus" or "Kyrie eleison." All the examples given are in foreign languages: sometimes it helps if the word used does not have mundane associations. Not many of us speak Aramaic around the house, so if we pray "Abba" (Father) or "Marána, tha!" (O Lord, come!) the sounds are unlikely to strum up distracting images. Those I have given are all sacred words: they come from the Scriptures or from the Christian liturgy. Once we are used to them they can become holy for us also, because they are a means of access to our own inner holy spaces.

If it happens that we are incurably vernacular and want to pray in English, we can take one of the words suggested in *The Cloud*, or we may like to hold on to a phrase from the Gospels, "My Lord and my God" (John 20:28) or some other. It is better not to make one up for oneself but to use a word given by a teacher, or drawn from the Bible or the liturgy. This is my word, one I can pray without reservation. It expresses where I feel I am before God at this moment.

The short prayer most favored among Eastern Christians is the "Jesus prayer": "Lord Jesus Christ, Son of God and Savior, have mercy on me, a sinner." This is a rich, composite text with many allusions to Gospel passages, comprising as well a balanced theology of Christ. It has a strong evangelical tone. Because it is a little longer than other examples, it will have to ride on several breaths instead of one. There are different attention-catching points within it. We may find that while the prayer is operating on automatic pilot, we focus on one single part that becomes almost its only feature. Today it may be the word "Lord" that absorbs me, and the rest of the prayer is like packing. Tomorrow it may be "mercy," and after that "sinner" or "Savior." The value of using this more complex prayer is that it offers variations interior to the prayer itself.

What gives specific flavor to any prayer is its being said from the heart in widely different circumstances. There is no reason for prayer to be any more monochromatic than life. Saint John Cassian advocated the use of the verse, "O God come to my assistance; O Lord make haste to help me," and devoted several paragraphs to showing how this simple text readily adapts itself to the most varied human situations – from headaches to temptations to the inpouring of grace by the Holy Spirit. Here is his summary:

> The prayer of this little verse is our constant and unceasing foundation: in adversity so that we may be rescued, in prosperity so that we may be kept safe and not allowed to become haughty. Let the quiet saying of this verse, I say, be carried on unceasingly in your breast. Do not cease from chanting it in any work or service or when you are going on a journey. Repeat it while sleeping and when taking your meals and even in the last necessities of nature [sic]. This movement of the heart will be for you, as it were, a formula to keep you safe; not only will it guard you unharmed from all demonic attack but it will also cleanse you from all the vices which follow upon worldly involvement and then it will lead you to the contemplation of unseen heavenly realities and to that unspeakable ardor of prayer which is experienced by only a few.

Let sleep come upon you as you recite this verse and, formed by unceasing exercise in it, let the habit of chanting it continue throughout sleep. Let this verse be the first thing to come to your mind on waking; let it precede every other conscious thought. Say it kneeling on getting up from your bed and let it accompany you in every task and activity and be with you all the time. Recite it according to the instructions of [Moses] the legislator: "sitting at home or walking on a journey," sleeping and rising. Place it on the lintel and door of your mouth, on the walls of your dwelling and in the sanctuary of your breast. In this way, when you prostrate in prayer this chant will bow down with you, and then, as you get up to give yourself to the customary actions which are necessary for life, the prayer will rise and continue with you.[5]

A short prayer used during meditation becomes Cassian's foundation for living mindful of the presence of God. He shows a preference for prayer that is short and frequent, rather than for prayer quarantined to one corner of the day. In this way prayer acts as an integrating agent, progressively pulling the disparate strands of one's behavior and thought into a unity under God. Then it feeds back into the practice of prayer. Most distractions in prayer are not due to external factors but to interior dividedness. To the extent we are brought into harmony, our prayer proceeds with less opposition. Saint John Climacus quotes a saying that prayer is the monk's mirror. In prayer we experience what we are: if single of heart, our prayer is strong like the current of a mighty river; if one's heart is racked with inconsistencies, one's prayer will be fluttery, like a moth against a window. Uniting prayer and daily experience means ultimately that we live more harmoniously and so prayer flows more surely.

There is another reason Cassian gives for short prayers – one that may seem a little bizarre. He envisages the mind as besieged by demons. The only way a message can be dispatched is to pass someone out through the gates before the demons know what is happening. If prayer is prolonged they have time to mount an offensive against it.

Prayer should, as it were, be hurriedly snatched from the jaws of the enemy while it is yet warm. For while he bothers us all the time, it is especially when he sees us praying to the Lord that he sets himself against us, activating different bodily factors in an effort to divert our minds from the intensity of prayer, and in this way attempting to make our prayer, which began warm, become cool. It was for this reason that they considered that the best way to pray was to pray briefly but often. If we frequently turn to God, then it is possible to remain close to him on a permanent basis. By framing our prayer in brief bursts we have the possibility of escaping the devil's darts, which assail us especially when we pray.[6]

We may smile at the primitivism of the language, but there is much practical wisdom behind it. If prayer is the search for the most profound level of our own being, then it is no shallow exercise. It is an entry into the realms of the unconscious. While we rightly hope to encounter God there, experience reveals that we meet other things as well. The explorer of inner space is liable to come across "monsters."

In the history of human malice – hatred, genocide, concentration camps, nuclear weaponry and all the other crimes that scar our memories – we find all come from one source, the human heart. Jesus alerted us to this (Mark 7:20–23). I am capable of participating in any of these crimes; the seeds of malice; blindness and weakness are within me. And the more I try to turn toward God, the more aware I become of this opposite tendency within me (see Romans 7:14–25). This sea of malice and spite has to be progressively reduced in the course of a lifetime. Handled prudently, the elimination of the vices need not be specially dramatic. Sometimes, however, one might give oneself too fervently to prayer, overstaying the natural limits and trying to force the issue. In that case one's system will try to redress the imbalance: instead of finding God we may find the devil, or (more properly) the daimonic within us. Usually this takes the form of temptation to the worst possible sins, according to what one believes are the worst possible sins: sexual sins, suicidal despair, blasphemy, apostasy from one's vocation, or whatever. Even if such temptations sometimes are successful, this should not cause panic. These events are simply manifesting something that has been latent. Nothing has changed except its degree of visibility. A little more prudence and discretion, and perhaps wiser direction, are indicated.

It *is* possible to go astray, but we should not become preoccupied with this. Often mistakes come from too much enthusiasm and too little common sense. Prayer spread consistently and gently throughout the day, as Cassian recommends, is on a sounder basis than if we try to pray for longer periods than our situation demands. If we do overindulge, it is our own fault if we get spooked.

Authentic prayer is such a subtle practice that it will not yield itself to any enthusiasm that is not spiritual, but merely a disguised form of a physical or emotional need. Again, *The Cloud* expresses the tradition of the centuries:

> Therefore, for God's love, be careful in this work and do not strain the heart in your breast by grossness or excess. Work more with a flair than with any gross strength. For the more lightly your work, the more humble and spiritual it is. The more gross, the more bodily and beastlike. Therefore be careful. Surely a beastlike heart that presumes to touch the high mountain of this work will be driven away with stones (Exodus 19:30) ... Therefore beware of this beastlike grossness and learn to love lightly with a soft and quiet countenance, as well in body as in soul. Wait for the Lord's will courteously and humbly; do not grab over-hastily, like a greedy greyhound, though your hunger is great.[7]

No method can supply for the unspirituality of our natural impulses; to pray well involves a long labor of refinement. The simplicity of a short prayer can hone the cutting edge of our spirits and thus advance our prayer.

Cassian makes another point about short prayers, namely that they are an expression of our poverty of spirit. Far from indicating an exuberant spiritual abundance, they reveal that prayer is only a faint whisper within us, and that even to pray briefly is impossible without God's grace.[8]

In the rosary we see the classical method of short prayers in a slightly different mode. Beads are used, as in many other religious traditions. There is some variety in the words used, but generally the prayer is consciously started and then left to continue under its own steam. Repeating the words gives a sense of tranquillity on one level, and greater direction to one's mind on another. The words provide a background to prayer that rises from the heart. Many find great help in praying this way, while others find the rosary a difficult prayer – mainly, I think, because they try too hard to "meditate" on the mysteries. If they were to start the words quietly and try to penetrate to the prayer within, matters would simplify. It might be better to say a single decade and then to rest in prayer, rather than forge ahead to make up the full tally of Hail Marys. Saint John Cassian makes a similar point:

> And so they think that it is more profitable to sing ten verses of a Psalm with attention than to pour forth the whole Psalm in a state of mental confusion such as may be generated when one hurries through the Psalm's recitation conscious only of the length and number of Psalms which remain to be sung. In such a case one is less interested in penetrating to the sense of what is sung than in quickly coming to the end of the service.[9]

In the rosary, as in every other form of prayer, gentleness and common sense go a long way to ensure that one's practice helps rather than hinders long-term growth in spiritual maturity and human interiority. If the rosary helps one to spend a quarter of an hour in quiet communion with God, it should be kept up. If it seems not to work at present, we should look for a substitute – something to help us to find our heart and maintain our search for God.

These three chapters have had as their theme various ways in which the Scriptures can animate our prayer: reflective reading, the use of familiar texts and the reciting of short prayers. It should be obvious that we need to keep enriching ourselves with all three, since each touches a different level of our spirit. As *The Cloud* expresses it:

> These are the means in which a contemplative apprentice should be occupied: lesson, meditation and orison, or else to your understanding they may be called: reading, thinking and praying.[10]

At different stages of life we need less of one and more of another: more reading, for example, to get us started as beginners; less reading when the habit of meditation is well-established. After years of progress we may have internalized God's Word to such an extent that books are rarely necessary. In general, however, all three elements need to be present to our lives in one form or another for a healthy practice of prayer.

Without exposure to God's Word, our prayer becomes stale and listless, and our inner life begins to revolve around points that are less relevant and engaging than they were previously. In that case it is time for fresh input. We also need to take time out to digest what we read, and live with the texts that engage us. So it is good as we pass through life's seasons to select a couple of theme songs that characterize each stage of growth, become familiar with them – perhaps even learn them by heart – and use them in prayer and at other times. Finally, one's practice of religion and fidelity to prayer will lack depth if one does not spend time in quiet communion with God.

In these ways we allow the inspired Word to refashion our lives so that they conform more closely to Christ's. To quote Cassian again: "Each hour and every moment we need to keep opening up the ground of our heart with the plough of the Gospel." The plough that breaks up surface hardness and provides access to the richer soil is the wisdom that comes "by the constant recalling of the Lord's cross."[11] When the meaning of the passion and resurrection of Jesus is alive within us we have greater fortitude in bearing with suffering. We also become aware of the inward power of the Spirit operating within our spirits and directing them toward God.

I conclude my remarks about short prayers with a brief quotation from Martin Luther:

> The right method is to use few words, but in many and profound meanings and senses. The fewer the words, the better the prayer. The more words, the worse the prayer. Few words and much meaning is Christian. Many words and little meaning is pagan.[12]

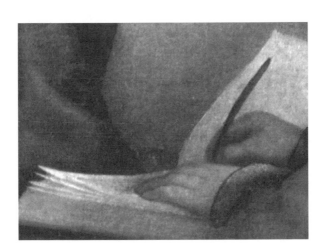

10

CREATING SPACE
FOR MEDITATION

"Meditation" is a fine-sounding word – not as up-market as "contemplation," but still with a certain ring to it. To remark airily that I spend time each day in meditation sounds more exclusive than confiding that I say my prayers. I fear meditation is becoming respectable, even fashionable. Some people may be attracted to it for the wrong reasons (which is no great problem, since meditation tends to sort us out). On the other hand others may hold back from meditation simply because it sounds too exalted.

In fact meditation is rather like respiration; we have probably been doing it all our lives without using the term. Meditating is "no big deal," or as the author of *The Cloud* put it when giving advice, "Travail steadfastly in this nought and in this nowhere."[1] At one level, meditation is precisely doing nothing; what we normally think of as skills and aptitudes are totally irrelevant to its practice.

> Your bodily wits may find there nothing to feed on. They think that you are doing nothing. Still keep on doing this nothing – provided you do it for love of God. Cease not but travail busily in that nothing with a conscious desire to want to have God, whom no human being can know. I tell you truly, I would rather be in this nowhere place, blindly wrestling with nothing than to be some great lord who could go where he wanted to and amuse himself with anything he liked.[2]

Prayer cannot be taught or learned, because it does not involve the application of conscious skills.

I think here of a great building in process of restoration. Often the major work involved is unlayering the accretions of the years and getting back to the original. The interior needs uncluttering. Those who formerly inhabited the building thought they were adding something by relieving its stark lines and making it "comfortable." In fact they were scaling down the original vision. The building was uncomfortable because it challenged them to grow; they put an end to that by changing its character and taming its forthrightness. And they were quite unaware of what they were doing.

To get to any level of truth of authenticity, we have to strip away much that is comfortable. We must approach prayer or meditation in a "ruthless" spirit. Time given to it will be wasted unless we are prepared to undercut our conventional assumptions about ourselves. We have to try to get beneath our ordinary level of behavior with its hopes and fears, punishments and rewards. We have to search out truth by putting aside, for the moment, all that clutters our minds and prevents us seeing what is underneath.

The task is simple in concept, but by no means easy. Prayer, in fact, is difficult; it is travail. The hardest part, however, is our own secret resistance to it. It is a permanent mystery to me why I do not pray more. I am attracted to prayer, and to the extent I do give myself to prayer I find myself more alive inwardly. Yet the simplest initiative toward prayer sometimes becomes more convoluted than getting a refund from a public official. I experience sudden inspirations about other things that need to be done, or an overwhelming wave of listlessness, or repugnance, or find my mind starting the kind of rational analysis that reduces everything to fine dust. I feel called to prayer, but at the same time find myself assailed by an astonishingly aggressive mood of inertia and reluctance.

There are two things I say to myself in such circumstances. First, this lack of responsiveness is not untypical. It mirrors the level of my resistance to God in all that I do – despite appearances to the contrary. This is the unpleasant truth: I withhold myself and will not be led where God desires me to go. So this is not just a matter of whether I pray now or not, but a larger question. The challenge of this moment is: Do I say "yes" to God or "no"? In some sense this petty incident asks me to state the direction I wish to give to my whole life. The fact that I dally before reaching a safe compromise, indicates accurately the substantial infidelity that characterizes my life as a whole at this period.

The second thing I say to myself is that if I did only what I felt like doing at the moment, I would have stopped getting out of bed several decades ago. I try to do those things I have decided in advance are good to do – to follow policies thought out previously. So I take precautions to ensure that my day is as I really want it to be. Once the important things are in place, lesser matters can be left to Providence, spontaneity, and perhaps even to caprice. As an individual, I need some structure in my day so that prayer is built into it in a way that reflects my present needs. Then I can relax and let everything else find its natural rhythm.

If I want to meditate, I have to find time for it. This means reviewing the normal pattern of my days and weeks, and finding slots that are practicable. Then I need to make a contract with myself, and perhaps with others who are affected by what I do, guaranteeing that these slots are left free for an initial period of a month or so. I monitor the result, perhaps discuss it with someone, and then, at the end of the agreed period, either renew and extend the contract, or make appropriate changes. I may even introduce a penalty clause that involves forfeiting some pleasure, rendering a service or paying a fine. That will test my seriousness. Sometimes games like this are helpful, so long as we do not become scrupulous about them. They give a certain visibility to the voice of conscience, which is otherwise interior and easily obscured.

It is good to pray when we feel inspired to, but it is the regular practice of prayer that takes us into the depths. In choosing slots for prayer we should be careful that they are not excessive; if they are tyrannical, our forces of resistance will double. Better to opt for a reasonable minimum in the hope that on good days we might extend it. All the experts suggest we meditate once a day at least, but I find it hard to be convinced by such arbitrary absolutes. Look at the week and select a few slots; keep to them, as best you can. If one feels a need to change the rhythm at the weekend, during an illness, on vacation or because of some extraordinary event, by all means do so. The structure chosen is for ordinary times; it is not written in the heavens. When circumstances change, our response to God's call to prayer will be expressed in different forms.

At this point, it may be useful to list a number of factors that can be of assistance as we go into meditation. There is a danger in doing so of giving the impression that one is compiling a list of prerequisites. On reading the list a person might say, "I don't fulfill the conditions even to make a start." So let me say at once that the list is simply an attempt to say what generally helps meditation go smoothly. Only rarely will *all* the items be possible; on most occasions we do the best we can in less than perfect circumstances. Still, it helps to know what the liabilities are: we may be able to do something to offset them.

AIDS TO MEDITATION

1. A regular time

2. Good physical health

3. Emotional equilibrium

4. Social harmony

5. Winding down

6. A suitable place

7. Good posture

8. Attention to breathing

I shall say something about each.

1. A regular time

We have already discussed how to choose times for meditation. The one aspect not yet addressed is duration. For what length of time should we pray? When growing into prayer, either for the first time or when making a fresh start, one might think of ten minutes or so, after settling in. A normal duration that suits many people is from fifteen to twenty minutes; this corresponds roughly to our attention span. If one is meditating for longer, it may help to break the period into small segments and take a minute or two for relaxation between them. One needs to experiment a little to find what is appropriate at the moment. There is no harm in going a little beyond our comfort zone, but we should avoid expecting too much of ourselves or turning meditation into an imposition. If we are underprayed, our tendency will be to make up the deficiency at another time; if, however, we are overprayed, we may experience disgust during meditation, and the thought of doing anything extra will probably not even occur. The only absolute rule regarding the duration of prayer is that each individual has to make a choice, based on prevailing circumstances.

2. Good physical health

Bodily indisposition can bring distractions during meditation, so it is good to be aware that one's powers of concentration are affected by one's physical health. The author of *The Cloud* wrote well about this point.

> I do not say that you can always continue in this work [of contemplation] with the same freshness. That is impossible. Sometimes sickness and other disordered dispositions in body and soul, with many other needs of nature, will hinder you greatly and often draw you down from the height of this work. What I do say is that you should always have this work in mind – in intention if not in fact. That is to say, either in work or in will. Therefore, for God's love, beware of sickness as much as you can, so that, as far as possible, it be not the cause of your feebleness. I tell you truly that this work demands a full great restfulness and a full whole and clean disposition as well in body as in soul. Therefore, for God's love, govern yourself discreetly in body and in soul and maintain your health as best you can.[3]

Meditation is not a licence for hypochondria, but it does demand that we be alert to self-destructive elements in our manner of life. As we enter more profoundly into the truth of our being, we may discover that certain avenues of gratification are progressively eroding our general vitality. We may come to see that we are continuing such activities less for the small joys they bring than because of habit and a fear that life would be less rich without them. If we plumb the depths of honesty, we may be forced to accept that there is an impulse toward self-destruction that makes us continue what we know to be harmful. We may, in fact, uncover a deep and mysterious vein of self-hatred. Meditation may come to grief through such an impulse, one that resists anything that works for our ultimate good. On the other hand, meditation is helped, indirectly, by anything that promotes a sense of health and well-being.

In spirituality there is a long history of mistrusting the body. This bias would not have clung so tenaciously if there were not some truth in it. But it is important to be convinced of the body's role in meditation. Some find that Hatha yoga postures or the movements of Tai Chi serve well in disposing them for meditation. Others prefer more conventional exercises or simply the variety of activities that make for a balanced day. Here, as elsewhere, the important thing is to accept responsibility for our own state – to take whatever measures are needed to promote health, irrespective of whether these are conventional or wildly unique.

This brings us to the question of asceticism. There is no doubt that physiological conditions influence what is experienced in meditation. Effects can be produced by going without food and sleep, as well as by factors on a more psychological level. In some traditions of meditation, physical abstention is regarded as essential if mental fireworks are to take place. Thus fasting and keeping night vigils are recommended. In Kundalini yoga there is a deliberate attempt to harness sexual energies to serve meditation, and this is at least implicit in traditions that inculcate celibacy or sexual restraint. I often feel a little guilty that I cannot feel more enthusiastic about the potential of such ascetical practices. I have no aversion to ecstasy, but would prefer to think it came from a full heart rather than from an empty stomach. Much depends on the dispositions of the person undertaking such practices, on whether there is a spiritual desire for God and a willingness to submit to the counsel of an experienced guide. On the other hand, there is no doubt that the opposite of asceticism – over-indulgence in food, drink, sex or anything else with the capacity to enslave us – has a disastrous effect on prayer and meditation. The pleasure principle has to be brought under control progressively; I doubt that it is prudent or possible to eliminate it altogether. For many of us it is more challenging to use creatively the gratifications life brings than to take the more dramatic step of renouncing them once and for all.

It helps if one comes to meditation relatively fresh – after the cleansing of a good night's sleep, or when a natural break occurs at the end of a block of activities, or even at the end of the day if we are not too tired. After a heavy meal one may well become drowsy while trying to meditate. We should, in any case, be confident that common sense will produce a practical solution, but a little effort may be needed to find it.

3. Emotional equilibrium

Unless one is vigilant, meditation time can be disrupted by rampant emotions. I am not suggesting we can turn our feelings on and off like a switch, but it is important to realize that strong emotions can torpedo prayer. But only if they operate out of control. When moving toward meditation, it is important to become aware of the feelings that are uppermost. Instead of trying to eliminate them, or allowing them to do what they like, I can turn to face them. We sit down together and talk about the situation, like adults. If I am angry, I must respect that anger and listen to it. I allow it to express itself and then I gently tease out what really is the source of the upheaval. I keep at this until I am able peacefully to see that – notwithstanding unfairnesses or even monstrous injustices – the cause of the anger is within me: in my sense of powerlessness, my fears, suspicions and loneliness. Once I have grasped what, within me, is reacting passionately to outward provocation, I can carry it into prayer. Not a replay of the battle but the root of my vulnerability, my fear or my loneliness. I begin: "Lord take pity on one so fearful" or "Lord take pity on one so lonely." Likewise with depression or sadness. "Why are you dejected, my soul? Why do you sigh within me?" (Psalm 43:5). We begin a dialogue with sadness to find its roots: laziness, bereavement, disguised anger or temptation. Again we carry the result to prayer. And lust? The same; but first translate it into human and personal terms, so that it fuels our prayer instead of quenching it.

In the mind of Saint John Cassian, anger and sadness are two principal preventatives of prayer: "The disturbance caused by anger or sadness is, above all things, to be eliminated at its sources."[4] The reason for such emphasis is simple. Both anger and sadness represent a refusal on our part to accept a situation that God's providence has allowed to develop. Whether our reaction is manic or depressive, we are expressing a lack of faith that in some way the present crisis is a gift from God, designed for our ultimate good. Taken far enough, even the most "innocent" annoyance becomes a doubt about God's love for us. Cassian says, when giving a commentary on the Lord's Prayer, "Nobody is able to say this prayer sincerely who does not believe that God's providence intends every situation, be it congenial or not, for good."[5]

Emotional balance is not easily achieved; we may have to learn to live with anger or depression for a long time before it is relieved. If it is not possible to get to the bottom of the negativity and overcome it, we might try an alternative tack. Without denying the emotion, try to inject its opposite. If one is sad, think of joy; if angry, turn to thoughts of peace. Saint Bernard of Clairvaux wrote:

> Therefore my advice to you, friends, is to turn aside from troubled and anxious reflection on your own progress, and escape to the easier paths of remembering the good things which God has done; in this way, instead of becoming upset by thinking about yourself, you will find relief by turning your attention to God ... Sorrow for sin is, indeed, a necessary thing, but it should not prevail all the time. It is necessary, rather, that happier recollections of the divine bounty should counterbalance it, lest the heart should become hardened through too much sadness and so perish through despair.[6]

Any one truth is not the whole truth; if we are in danger of being submerged by a partial truth, the remedy is to cling to its opposite. If the justice of God fills me with dread, it is time to turn and consider divine mercy. If I am sad about something I do not have, I give thanks for all I have been given.

4. Social harmony

The words of our Lord cannot be ignored: "And when you are praying, let go if you have something against anyone in order that your Father in heaven may let go of your transgressions for you" (Mark 11:25). I translate the verb in this saying as "let go" rather than "forgive" or "remit." So long as I cling to another's fault, I perpetuate it. The malice has left the other person and now lives in me. True, I have been wronged, perhaps thoughtlessly, perhaps with deliberate intent. Yet I am a victim in a more profound sense, because evil passed from the other to me. What was expressed momentarily in an action or a series of actions is now enshrined in my unforgiving heart. Until I let go my grievance the malice remains active. Whenever I make space for God in my heart, it will invade.

In the Our Father we pray, "Forgive us as we forgive" (Matthew 6:12). All prayer is a process of letting go past grievances. Seldom easy, rarely instantaneous, but always necessary. One does not go far on the journey of meditation before becoming aware that the ability to meditate is closely allied to one's willingness to be at peace with all. Maybe the obstacle is a figure from our past, someone who abused our trust in childhood or afterward. Perhaps someone who is the innocent victim of our projections. Or maybe it is a rival, an unneighborly neighbor, someone temperamentally distant from us, someone who is withholding love. Such a person we must forgive. We must not clasp to our hearts the sin we impute to the other; we have to let it go. And then see what happens.

We need to dialogue with our antipathies, as with our other feelings, to learn their cause. From that we pray. As we make efforts to reduce discord in daily life, we become reconciled to our irretrievable past and learn to think more kindly about those who have wronged us. We may well come to realize we are not as blameless as we first assumed. We may also have to discover how to forgive ourselves. Meditation is the way to peace: through persevering in it we are forced to confront and undo whatever keeps us apart from other human beings.

5. Winding down

I do not speak about preparation for meditation, because this sounds like staging a dress rehearsal before the curtain goes up. I prefer to speak of letting go or winding down, gradually dismissing anything that would clutter up the space into which I will invite the Lord.

The best illustration of what is involved is the process of going to sleep at night. Nothing is worse than trying too hard, or reading books about insomnia. Ideally we drift into sleep on automatic pilot. We gradually leave aside the concerns of the day, put into operation whatever routines are preludes to rest, and then let nature take its course. We avoid excitement and postpone difficult decisions. Our first priority is restoration of energies through a good night's sleep. Things will look better in the morning.

The author of *The Cloud* writes in another work about similarities between meditation and sleep:

> And well is this work likened to a sleep. For as in sleep the use of the bodily wits ceases so that the body may take its full rest in the feeding and strengthening of its bodily nature, so in spiritual sleep, the wanton questions of the wild spiritual wits and the reasonings of the imagination are bound fast and utterly voided so that the simple soul may softly sleep, and resting in the lovely beholding of God as he is, in the full feeding and strengthening of the spiritual nature.[7]

The nature of contemplative meditation determines what conditions facilitate it. Because it is beyond images, concepts and thoughts, none of these is useful. The best preparation is gradually emptying the mind. This can take a few moments before meditation. Why not have one's distractions in peace?

In fact distractions during meditation are more avoidable than is generally recognized. More about this later. For now, I simply note that one generator of thoughts during attempts at prayer is the unprocessed state of our daily experiences. Living pressurized lives, we pass through a series of high-tension situations, butted one against another. There is no opportunity to process life as it happens. We schedule the day so that no time is lost. From work we move into hectic traffic; and for relaxation we play competitive sports or turn to images and sounds from the media. There is little time to come to grips with what we are experiencing. As we try to clear our minds for meditation, all the unprocessed experience comes tugging at our emotions. What is needed is time to empty the garbage: chalk up some matters to experience, laugh out loud or to blush with embarrassment – then file the rest away for future action. Then meditation runs more smoothly – and perhaps we may later sleep more deeply.

As time goes by, one may come to exercise greater vigilance over what one thinks about. Non-repressive control of thoughts can be useful, not only to keep one's system clearer for meditation, but also to channel one's mental energies toward more creative goals. Cassian comments:

> Whatever thoughts our mind conceives before the time of prayer will certainly re-occur in the memory during prayer. For this reason we should try to prepare ourselves before the time of prayer by being the sort of person we would wish to be during prayer.
> The mind is shaped during its prayer by what it was beforehand. When we prostrate ourselves in prayer, our previous actions, words and impressions continue to play before the minds of our imagination, just as they did before, making us angry or sad, or causing us to relive past lusts or foolish laughter. I am ashamed to admit that we are even entertained by comic words and deeds and our mind is diverted by recalling conversations we have had previously.
> It is because of this that, before prayer, we ought to be quick to exclude from the approaches to our heart anything that would

disturb our prayer. In this way we can fulfil the saying of the Apostle, "Pray without ceasing." And "In every place lifting up our hands without anger or quarrelling." It is not possible to put his injunction into practice in any other way. We must see that our mind is cleansed from the poison of every vice and that it gives itself, as to its natural object, to be fed by the continual contemplation of almighty God.[8]

Because it is generally not possible to control events to the extent Cassian thought advisable, most of us will have to struggle with unwanted imaginings. We can certainly try to empty the mind in advance – even taking a short walk can accomplish this sometimes, or relaxing in an armchair, or listening to music. It does not matter what we do as long as we appreciate that one cannot rush into meditation without quieting down. Otherwise most of the time will be spent not in finding one's heart but in coping with the contents of one's head.

6. A suitable place

Those of us who belong to the lower classes, and do not have a basilica in the backyard, should give special thought to finding a suitable place for meditation. Ideally one returns to the same place or places regularly. The Gospel speaks of praying from "an inner room" (Matthew 6:6). We may choose our own bedroom, or another room if there is one spare. Part of the strategy may include finding a time when part of the house is unused, and making the most of that opportunity. Unless one has access to a church one will have to exercise some ingenuity to discover somewhere that helps rather than hinders prayer.

Environment is important. One's inner state often reflects the conditions around. We are not pure spirits; feeling is affected by what impinges on our senses. A space that is quiet and uncluttered is generally a great help. The very act of entering that space and shutting the door will induce a sense of tranquillity in which prayer appears more readily.

Some like to give their location a sacred meaning by introducing an object signifying its purpose: a cross, an icon that appeals to us, or a lighted candle. We could burn incense if this does not attract hostile attention from others. These are minor matters but they do give a distinctive character to the environment – and also attest to our seriousness about meditation. Each must find a nook suitable for the work.

7. Good posture

Many of us were brought up under the impression that the body contributes little to the quality of meditation. In reality, nothing could be further from the truth. Many problems in prayer derive from bad posture. And any care invested in arriving at a position that promotes stillness of body and directedness of mind is well worth the effort. Think of meditation as a bodily action. We need a posture that enables us to remain calm and still but not sleepy. A relaxed yet disciplined posture.

Here one is again talking about individual possibilities. Fifteen years ago I found two yoga positions very helpful, the lotus posture and the so-called perfect posture. They contributed greatly to a sense of integration. They seemed to bring bodily energies together so that I was able to pray relatively undistracted for as long as I liked. I am not sure why or when I stopped using them, but I have not assumed them as prayer postures for some years. Nowadays I tend to kneel and sit back on my heels, with a small cushion supporting my ankles. I find this, at the moment, completely satisfactory – though I would prefer not to be so dependent on the cushion. I offer my own experience here simply to show that everyone must search around for something that helps, and to underline the fact that as one gets older one may lose some agility.

The paramount element of good posture is keeping the spine straight. To slump or slouch is not only externally ugly, but seems to interfere with one's inner sense of being physically together, of doing something and not just letting time pass. Whether one sits or kneels or uses a prayer-stool makes no great difference, so long as one's back is straight – not in a military way, as if one had swallowed a poker, but in a calm natural way. It may take a little muscular re-education for some, but the result is worth it. Good posture is at the heart of simple, objectless meditation.

In fact so little is happening on an external level that the body becomes the focus of our effort to pray. One remains quietly before the Lord; and once the mind is disengaged, only the flickering pilot light of one's posture gives the slightest indication of activity.

Posture is an expression of our prayer. In its own body language, the physical organism unites with the heart in turning toward God. By keeping still, we renounce busyness. By unity and directedness of posture, we express determination to unite all our powers in seeking God. By being on the floor, we signal putting aside our executive self-image, simply conscious of being before God in utter humility.

To make a gesture with the hands can add further meaning to posture. Joining the hands is an almost universal expression of prayer. It also promotes a restful feeling that spreads through the whole body. Try it. Fingers are among the most sensitive tactile parts of the body; when they are put together, there is a sense of balance and harmony. Alternatively, we may open our hands in the traditional Christian gesture still used in the liturgy. This can also speak volumes. Again, we may choose to rest the open palms together, or join thumb and forefinger as was done previously in the Latin liturgy – and as is much favored by Tibetan Buddhists "keeping the thumbs warm." Hands should be invited to join in our meditation.

And one's eyes too. Some find it helpful to close their eyes; this is good since it reduces the possibility of external distractions. It does cause problems for some because of drowsiness, and for others because closed eyes stimulate the visual imagination, whereas with eyes open, they cannot be distracted by visual images. With eyes open, or perhaps half-open, we may like to focus on an object one or two meters in front, such as a cross or a candle. This prevents one's gaze from sauntering round the room. If the focus has a sacred character, there may be an exchange of energies between it and the one who meditates: the meditator has a sense of being drawn toward it, through it and beyond it. In Catholic tradition this function was often filled by the tabernacle or the monstrance; these served to fix one's attention and direct it to God.

I want now to say something about the sacrament of sound. If circumstances allow, and we care to try it, we may say our short prayer aloud, allowing it to echo in the ears as well as in the heart. This has a number of benefits. A word pronounced concentrates the mind and dispels alternative thoughts more effectively than a word merely thought. We have the chance also to prolong the syllables in accord with our breathing. One may even sing. The *Kyrie eleison* sung in Gregorian melody is a powerfully moving prayer which for certain people expresses their own prayer more profoundly than any spoken word. Here, as elsewhere, I do no more than alert the reader to a possibility. You must judge whether a particular suggestion has relevance to your own particular situation and to the kind of prayer with which you feel at home.

8. Attention to breathing

Most of the bodily changes associated with emotion do not come under the direct control of the will. Generally we have little control over whether we blush or blanch, or whether our blood pressure rises or falls. But it is possible to exercise voluntary control over our breathing – which is also affected immediately in emotional excitement. By attending to our breathing we can do something to lower our stress levels and to induce throughout the whole organism greater relaxation.

Many people find attention to breathing a helpful preparation for prayer; others maintain it distantly throughout their meditation. One simply takes a few moments to become aware of the present rate of breathing; then, gently, moves toward a deeper, slower and calmer rhythm. Of more esoteric techniques I have no desire to speak here, except to say that they are best practiced under a wise supervisor.

It may be helpful for the reader if I now translate all that has been said here into a kind of script for a meditation session under ideal circumstances.

> After giving myself time to *slow down* and clear my head for meditation, at the regular time I go to my *prayer place* and assume my *posture.*
>
> ✣
>
> After a moment I make a formal *beginning* with the Sign of the Cross or a brief opening prayer, or by some other means. Then I recite slowly and reverently the *short prayer* which I have selected. I do not think about its meaning or try to analyze its contents; I simply give myself to saying it and repeat it a few times.
>
> ✣

After some time I may notice the prayer tending to slow itself down. If I am using a longer text, one part may begin to stand out more strongly than the rest. I should devote most of my attention to this.

✛

I try to feel the prayer as coming from my heart, as coming from the situation in which I find myself before God, and I allow it to lead me. I follow. I do not fear.

✛

Without becoming too self-conscious I allow the sense of spiritual presence to strengthen. I do or say whatever seems to reinforce that sense and I withdraw from anything that weakens it.

✛

I allow the prayer to act as my guide.

✛

If other thoughts come along, I leave them aside gently, no matter how holy or useful they appear – even if they seem to be important insights. Now is not the time. If they persist, I remove them from sight by starting the short prayer again.

✛

As time goes on, I will learn to gauge the length of my prayer; in the meantime, I should be content to pass in and out of deeper prayer until I have a sense that my prayer is complete or that the time has elapsed.

✛

I gently wind matters up. Perhaps I close with a formal prayer or add some word of intercession. Then I wait for a few moments and withdraw.

There is nothing particularly complicated about this procedure, although writing it down may make it appear so. The outline above is intended as an illustration only. In fact most people make their own distinctive changes, and rarely are any two periods of prayer alike. The great problem with this sort of prayer is its simplicity. It has no entertainment value. There is virtually nothing to do except to sit still and allow the Spirit to be active on our behalf. It is not quietism, because we are very busy remaining quiet; and once we feel ourselves responding, we know this is more than a pious void. The format itself is not limited to people who are "advanced" (whatever that means). It is a quite ordinary way of spending time trying to be open to God's interior drawing. God is the agent in prayer; we are the recipients.

If praying in this blind, naked way is attractive, it is worth pursuing. If it seems a waste of time, it is better forgotten. However, it is worthwhile knowing that such an approach to prayer exists. Some time in the future one may feel drawn to it, or something like it, and it is helpful to know in advance that it is a perfectly normal development.

Different personality types will use different proportions in blending the elements discussed, or need more of one help than of another. Someone of a temperament opposite to mine might always prefer an alternative approach. I offer these concrete suggestions in the hope that someone may be helped by having them recorded in detail.

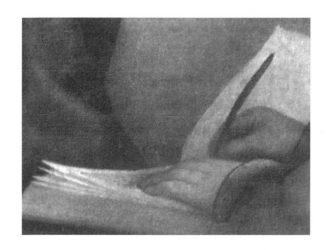

11

SOMETIMES...

In the Latin tradition of writing about the experience of prayer, there is a word that indicates a shift in the prevailing mood. That word is "sometimes." True, the practice of meditation requires dedication and discipline. True, prayer is often laborious and unrewarding. But *sometimes* it is not.

Prayer can easily seem a rather grim reality – a matter of facing up to the truth about ourselves, plumbing the depths of our bad faith and striving to re-educate ourselves to live by the Gospel. The results can seem meager. We seek, perhaps with a great deal of industry, but do not seem to find God. I come to prayer to give my time to God but the question that bothers me is: "Should I be experiencing more than this?" "Where," I ask "are the illuminations and consolations others speak about so rapturously?"

These are good questions, easier to answer on an individual basis than in general. Certainly the effects of prayer become apparent only after a time. What one feels at the end of a particular session need not reflect the cumulative value of what has been done over months. What one should expect has two aspects: a more acute sense of dissatisfaction with the less desirable aspects of one's life, together with a mysterious sense of contentment that is harder to budge – a feeling of "something going on" inside, and a growing belief that one is drawn toward God. The two experiences seem to be opposites; in fact they are pulling in the same direction, though in different manners. One breaks our complacency, the other reminds us that ultimately only God can bring us happiness.

The feelings are not boisterous but very sober. The dissatisfaction we feel is not the gnawing regret of an uneasy conscience or the expectant ache of a badly programmed superego. It is a mellow, undramatic recognition of the liabilities in one's life. It is not depressive but may even include a touch of whimsy – and it is eminently realistic. One might call it "humility," if that word does not connote an unhealthy depreciation of self or an undue measure of timidity. The sense of contentment is also sober rather than enthusiastic. In the early stages, it may not be openly religious. The feeling is that, despite one's unworthiness and low level living, there is a deep affinity with spiritual things – that there is a segment of oneself that comes alive when one is turned toward God. Neither experience is likely to generate instantaneous changes in one's life. Their accumulation is like dropping pennies in a bottle. Imperceptibly a reserve accumulates that one day impels me to take the step I would previously have judged beyond my capabilities.

Spiritual experience has a dual nature: it is both attraction to God and detachment from sin. It is not always recognized that the positive element, being drawn toward God, has to come first. No matter how disgusting our sins, we show little interest in giving them up unless something better offers. Then we generally lose interest in what satisfied us previously. One never lets go of the things that bring comfort until one lays hold of something better; then change is instantaneous and painless. The first stage in most conversions is a deep sense of joyful discovery. In the light of this one is happy to allow one's sins to slip away.

There is a passage of Saint Gregory the Great's describing how this dynamic works. It is no sudden process, rather a gradual modification of attitude. We return to our vices repeatedly, but with each relapse there is less satisfaction. We continue only through habit. Progressively we yearn to be quit of them.

> *Sometimes* one is admitted to a particular, unaccustomed experience of inner sweetness and is, in some way, a new creature, set afire by the breath of the Spirit. The more one tastes the object of love, the stronger grows one's desire for it. Within oneself one craves what one has experienced through the inner sense of taste and, from love of that sweetness, becomes of less value in one's own eyes. *After one has discovered that sweetness one becomes able to perceive what sort of a person one is without it.* One tries to prolong the experience, but is driven back from its strength because one is still weak. And being incapable of contemplating such purity, one weeps sweet tears and falls back and lies down on the tears of one's weakness. For the eye of the mind is unable to fix itself on what it had so fleetingly glimpsed. It is subject to the constraint of inveterate habit which holds it down. In this state one is filled with yearning and ardently tries to transcend oneself,

but each time one is beaten by fatigue and falls back into the
familiar darkness. A soul so moved must endure a serious inner
struggle against itself.[1] *[Emphases mine.]*

Dissatisfaction with one's present performance increases as one is
convinced something better is possible. This is the opposite of self-
depreciation. Glimpsing our potential we become somewhat bitter,
because inertia causes it to remain dormant. Then progressively one
is weaned from vices and becomes freer to follow the spiritual
attraction – though the process is never complete. For most, wavering
between the two extremes continues till the very end.

In his spiritual teaching, Saint Bernard of Clairvaux emphasized
this process of alternation. In a key text he notes that the Spirit seems
to come and go in our hearts, and suggests this is to permit us to
discover what we are like left to our own devices. The Spirit returns
so that we experience again the infinite possibilities opened up by
grace – and become more aware of the source of all spiritual energies.

> Therefore we must remain alert, alert at all times, since we can
> never know in advance when the Spirit comes and when he goes.
> For it is a fact that the Spirit does come and go and that the human
> being who stands with his support must fall when this support is
> withdrawn. But the collapse is not total, since the Lord, once
> again, stretches out to him a helping hand.
>
> For people who are spiritual or, rather, for those whom the Lord
> intends to make spiritual, this process of alternation goes on all
> the time. God visits by morning and subjects to trial. One who is
> righteous falls seven times and seven times gets up again. What is
> important is that the fall occurs during the day so that one sees
> oneself falling and knows that one has fallen and wants to get up
> again and so cries out for a helping hand saying, "O Lord at your
> will you made me splendid in virtue, but then you turned away
> your face and I was overcome."[2]

A person on the way toward God cannot expect continual progress or
unwavering determination. We wobble along the journey, stumble off
the path, find ourselves attracted in other directions, stand still, even
regress. This is almost universal experience. What is significant is the
strength of the reflex that keeps us bouncing back. There is
something we keep returning to: a vision, a dream, a hope. Some-

thing gives us the courage to get up after each fall and resume the journey. This is concrete evidence of the Spirit's work, far more potent than any spiritual euphoria.

Some experiences that keep us moving toward God are known only in their effects. Others are more accessible. A feeling arises from one's heart at prayer, or at some other time, that instantly radiates throughout one's being. It is like the sun breaking through on a cold spring day. There is light, warmth and a sense of well-being. Winter seems well past and there is promise of better days ahead. Even if clouds soon return, the glow of hope remains sufficient for now to keep us going.

Useful comment on this apparent withdrawal of grace and its subsequent return is found in *The Cloud of Unknowing*:

> I do not say that for those called to this work [the feeling of grace] will last forever and dwell in their minds continuously. It is not so. For the actual feeling is often withdrawn from a young novice in this work for various reasons. Sometimes to avoid familiarity, thinking that it is within one's own power to have it at will. Such a way of thinking is pride. Whenever the feeling of grace is withdrawn, pride is the cause ... Sometimes the feeling is withdrawn for their negligence. In such cases they quickly feel a bitter pain that bites them and hurts. In other cases our Lord will delay the feeling of grace by a ruse. By so dealing with them their desire grows and they esteem more what had been lost when it is newly found and felt again. This is one of the clearest and compelling signs that a soul may have to know if it be called to this work: if it feel after such a delaying and a long lacking of this work that when it comes suddenly, unpurchased by any means, that it has a great fervor of desire and more love and longing for this work than ever before. Often, I believe, there is more joy in finding than ever there was sorrow in losing. And if this be so, then this is an unmistakable sign that such persons are called by God to work in this work, whatever they now are or had been in the past.[3]

Our relationship with God changes. It is a rich dialectic of presence and absence, each phase representing a facet of the whole. We rejoice in the presence of the One who has attracted our love, we are sad when the One loved is absent. The truth is that God is neither totally present nor totally absent in our lives. It is right that our prayer experience should reflect this duality.

Beyond this daily alternation, there are longer-lasting variations in one's spiritual climate. It is good to recognize these also. They are like the seasons. If I were totally isolated, I might wonder why I feel colder at one time, why all the plants and trees seem to die, why the sun doesn't shine and the clouds pour down rain. I might surmise that it was due to something in me – something I had done or omitted that had lost me the favor of the elements. I might lose hope. But if I lived long enough, a pattern would begin to emerge; I would learn to distinguish the qualities of each season, discover how to deal with each and prepare for the coming of the next.

Our lives follow patterns, though these are not as predictable as the seasons. The problem about having a rigid rule of life that is meant to last from here to eternity is that it will probably not work. About half the time it will impose a burden that crushes one's spirit instead of teaching it to fly. For much of the remainder it lets the person off too easily, so that one does not realize one's full potential. We need to adapt our way of living to the way we are now, not the way we were a few months ago. We need to take stock, gauge our spiritual climate and design an appropriate way of living.

There have been long periods in my life when prayer came fairly easily, and it did not seem difficult to maintain a good relationship with God or try to carry out God's will. There have been other times when I seemed to be in a neutral phase, living on the strength of good habits, not getting into much mischief but mostly attending to areas in my life other than the spiritual. There have been times, too, when prayer was an experience of great anxiety and dread, sometimes because a specific decision was demanded of me and at other times for reasons more mysterious than that. At other times again, prayer was neither easy nor difficult, simply because nothing was further from my mind. Apart from customary prayers endured in boredom or in a riot of distractions, I carried on pretty much on my own for a time, cheerfully allowing God to go one way while I went mine. I was shocked sometimes by how far I seemed to have strayed, but was always confident of my ability to find the path again.

I do not claim these "seasons" are normative or universal, but they are ones I have experienced. Much of their significance is seen only in retrospect. I would not try to score each of them for their contribution to my spiritual growth, since I believe each one of them has been invaluable. I would not want to have been unrelievedly fervent, because for me that would have been inauthentic. I would not have wanted to live out years saturated with dread, but my negative experience in prayer has been more fruitful than all the days of sunshine. I am glad other areas of my life have not been neglected even though they have drawn energy away from "spirituality." And my sorry tale of infidelities serves as a reminder of what I do not want to become. Each season has held its own grace, in God's providence, and I cannot prefer one to another. Nothing God has made, or allowed, ever loses its potential to contribute to one's ultimate welfare.

We need to be patient and not expect the good things from all the seasons to be quickly gathered into one. Each has negative and positive features; these we need to identify so as to deal with them creatively. Good features may have to co-exist with vices because we are not yet ready for the latter's removal. Something similar applies to our dealings with others. Patience is needed: we cannot anticipate the time of another's conversion. As Saint Augustine advised, "Let us not forget what we were once and then we will not lose hope for those who are now what we used to be."[4]

In brief, we should not allow ourselves to be tyrannized by expectations about what we should be experiencing. If it is winter within, I should not punish myself for a lack of warmth. For a time I will be living at a level of reduced efficiency. My responses to some situations may be exaggerated: I may become so involved with my own hardship that I cease to be aware of what others expect from me or wish to give me. I may resent it when friends are lighthearted. Some elements in my situation will simply have to be endured. Others I must try to modify. For a time I may have to "fake it" for the sake of others dependent on me. All of this means recognizing the state in which I find myself, doing my best to minimize its liabilities – and making the most of whatever assets are hidden beneath the surface.

A person living realistically from day to day, accepting each moment as God's gift, comes to the point of harboring few expectations. What develops is one's capacity to be surprised. It is not only that the predictable lacks interest: when everything is sewn up, God tends to be excluded. When one conceives and organizes projects, there is always a danger of overlooking the unseen factor. So inevitably – and mercifully – the shell we have formed is cracked open by a reality too ample to be confined.

There are surprises in our prayer also – pleasant surprises. I have discussed at length the negative aspects of prayer, its difficulties, the dread it can arouse and its lack of tangible satisfactions. It is not abnormal to experience such things. But prayer is also a source of comfort and strength, a consolation in times of trouble, the mind's flowering and the will bearing fruit. It is finding one's heart and meeting with God. Once could not embrace prayer and its burdens if it were devoid of such affirmative results. We persevere, secretly sustained at a level deeper than feeling, with an inkling God awaits us ahead.

And sometimes prayer catches fire. We become aware of a burning love for God present with us. We can become so absorbed as to lose contact with our surroundings, and time seems to have no reality. The body, the mind and the spirit cease to be external to one another and instead coalesce in a single concentrated stream of energy directed toward God. We sense ourselves distantly as being totally alive. There may even be experience of oneself as a kind of a whirlpool that draws into its depths any who approach it. For a startling moment one may have a sense of identification with all humanity – all being carried, willy-nilly, toward God.

In such moments, prayer seems to be a kind of cosmic communion, a sort of metaphysical adventure. At other times, prayer may have a far more interpersonal quality about it, overwhelmed by what Julian of Norwich is wont to call the "homeliness" of God: how near, how accessible, how friendly, how unawesome God is. In many ways this is a stronger experience than the previous one. It relates more readily to our ordinary categories of consciousness and we are able to ponder on it afterward, enjoying its lingering aftertaste of love and benevolence. With time, the experience feeds into our behavior and makes us gentler.

The traditional image that unites these metaphysical and interpersonal experiences is spiritual marriage. Many people find such language difficult to accept, mainly because it is often used inaccurately. There is currently a distaste for nineteenth-century prayer books abounding in imagery of the "languishing spouse"; their inauthenticity is now repulsive to most. But the image itself can be traced back to classical sources, at least as far as Origen. The bridegroom is the Word. The bride is twofold; she may be the Church *(Ecclesia)* or she may be the individual soul *(anima)*, both realities being conceived of as feminine. One must be careful here. The bridegroom is the Word, rather than Jesus Christ. At the level of contemplative experience there is no image of the physical body of Christ. The conjunction is at the level of the spirit and the will. There is no reference to visions or imaginative constructions, but only to a marriage of wills. This is stated clearly by Saint Bernard:

> Such conformity marries the soul to the Word. She who is like him by nature now shows herself like him by an act of the will, loving in the same way that she is herself loved. Therefore, if she loves perfectly she has been married.
>
> What can be a source of greater pleasure than such a close union of wills? What can be more desirable than the love by which you, O soul, are not satisfied with human teaching, but go directly to the Word, remaining joined to the Word, familiarly relating and discussing whatever falls within the mind's grasp and the range of bold desire.
>
> Such a soul has really entered a spiritual and holy contract of marriage. Perhaps instead of "contract" I should say "contact" since there is here, without doubt, question of an embrace. This is because when two will the same things and reject the same things, they become one spirit.[5]

The resulting union is at the level of the spirit, a knitting together of the human and the divine wills sometimes symbolized by an exchange of hearts. Whether the experience is authentic can easily be verified by examining the person's daily conduct. Unlike other contemplative experiences occurring in people at all stages of growth, spiritual marriage seems to presuppose a substantial and sustained fidelity to the will of God in the details of ordinary living. Whether or not the image itself is used is immaterial, since at the level where it occurs bridal trappings are relatively unimportant. All that matters is love.

Even if we have little use as yet for spiritual marriage imagery, we can still benefit from the image of lovers seeking to give and receive love. The Song of Songs has been used repeatedly by great spiritual teachers of the church as an allegory of the soul's relationship with

God. It in fact lays a foundation for developing the theme of presence and absence. When the bridegroom is absent, the bride is drawn to seek him; when he arrives, her days of sorrowing are over and great rejoicing begins.

There are beautiful passages in Bernard's seventy-fourth sermon on the Song of Songs, where he speaks with great passion about the bridegroom's arrival and departure:

> You might ask, therefore, how it is that I know that the Word has arrived, since all his ways are beyond scrutiny. I know because he is living and active. As soon as he arrives within he shakes my sleepy soul into life. He moves and softens and pierces my heart which had previously been hard, stony and twisted out of shape. The Word begins to root up and destroy, to build up and to plant. He waters the arid soil and enlightens the gloom; he opens up what was closed and inflames what was frigid. At the same time he makes the twisted roads straight and the rough pathways smooth. And all this is done so that my soul may bless the Lord and all that is within me may give thanks to his holy name.
>
> So it is that, when the bridegroom comes to me, as *sometimes* he does, he never signals his presence by any token, neither by voice nor by vision nor by the sound of his step. By no such movement do I become aware of him, nor does he penetrate my being through the senses. Only by the movement of my heart, as I have already said, do I come to realize that he is with me. It is by the expulsion of my vices and the suppression of carnal feelings that I become aware of the might of his power. I am lost in wonderment at the depths of his wisdom when he subjects my inner life to scrutiny and correction. It is from a slight improvement in my behavior that I experience his goodness. It is from the reformation and the renovation of the spirit of my mind, that is, of my inner self, that I perceive his beauty and attractiveness. From the consideration of all these together, I come to be overwhelmed by his great kindness.
>
> He does not come in through the eyes, for he has no color; nor through the ears, since he makes no sound. It is not through the nose that he comes since he mingles not with the air but with the mind; to the atmosphere he gives being not odor. He does not gain entry through the mouth, since he is not food or drink. He cannot be contacted through touch since he is impalpable. How, then, does he find entrance?
>
> Perhaps he does not "come" at all, since he does not enter from

the outside, nor is he an external object. But, on the other hand, neither does he come from inside me since he is good, and I know that inside me there is nothing good.

I ascended to what was highest in my soul and, lo, the Word loomed loftier. I descended to the depths and found that he was yet deeper. If I looked out, I saw him beyond my outer limits. If I gazed within, more inward yet was he. It was then that I realized the truth of what I had read, "In him we live and move and have our being." Happy is the soul in whom dwells the One by whom she lives; happy the soul who lives for and is moved by such a One.

And when it happens that the Word departs, it is as though you were to remove the fire from beneath a boiling pot. Immediately it turns lifeless and stops boiling and begins to get cold. For me, this is the sign of his departure. My soul necessarily feels sad until his return when he again, as usual, reheats my heart within me. For this is the sign of his coming back.[6] *[Emphasis mine.]*

The overriding impression is of a visitation of the Word that is not traceable to any action on one's own part – yet through it one comes alive. The Word is the life of the soul. This contemplative experience is not an exaltation of the self. It is, on the contrary, self-forgetfulness. Bernard adverts to this in a passage written shortly before his death:

> *Sometimes* there is an experience of ecstasy or a recession from bodily senses because *the soul becomes so aware of the Word that is it no longer aware of itself.* This happens when the mind, enticed by the unimaginable sweetness of the Word is, somehow, stolen from itself. It is seized and snatched away from itself so that it may find pleasure in the Word.[7]

One who has progressively displaced self as the center of gravity in daily living experiences the same displacement in prayer. Even those in whom the process has just begun may be encouraged by experiencing how pleasurable it is to move out, and let God move in.

But be warned. All the great teachers insist that the positive contemplative experience is infrequent and of short duration. "What a pleasurable exchange," writes Saint Bernard, "yet what a short moment and what a rare experience!"[8] The more it is sought for its own sake, the more it is delayed. It is given only to those who seek God and willingly walk the ways of darkness. Those still in the business of self-exaltation will find themselves excluded. This is so because in a curious way contemplative experience fills one with an overwhelming sense of the generosity and condescension of God. One becomes more and more aware of one's own unworthiness and of one's spirit being little more than a void waiting to be filled. There is not much to boast of in a void.

> When a candle burns you can see by its light both the candle itself and other things, so when your soul burns in the love of God (i.e. when you feel your heart continually desire the love of God) then by the light of grace sent into your reason, you may hope to see both your own unworthiness and God's great goodness. And therefore, cleanse your mirror and proffer your candle to the fire.[9]

"Proffer your candle to the fire!" From the moment of our creation we are meant for enlightenment; nothing we do or fail to do can change this. True happiness and growth toward God consist in taking a thousand small steps toward illumination. We reach out our tiny candle toward the immense fire of divine love and allow ourselves to receive its light. No matter that we appear so small, we have become sources of light.

At times one may be overwhelmed by the extent to which turning toward God involves negative experience. We can grow tired of pain and endurance and courage and truth. Their hard edges afford us little comfort. We are puzzled by Saint Augustine's frequent assertion that there is only one way to God: the way of delight. The negative stages of growth remove one's substitute sources of satisfaction – perhaps taken without our having any say in the matter. This is a hard road, but the only way to become more sensitive to the subtler awakenings marking our journey toward God. In a darkened room we see only blackness at first. If we stay, our eyes adapt and we begin to work harder at the task of perception. Moreover, there is a quality of night vision that is lost when the lights go on. Some re-education of our sensibilities is necessary before exposure to the infinitely pleasing mystery of God. And detachment is the almost automatic effect in one whose inner tastes have changed. Saint Gregory the Great remarks:

> One who has come to know perfectly the sweetness of the heavenly life happily leaves behind everything previously loved on

earth. In comparison with this, everything else is devalued. One abandons one's possessions and scatters what has been amassed since one's soul is on fire for heavenly things and has no pleasure in the things of earth ... What previously brought pleasure to one's soul now becomes an intolerable burden.[10]

And:

If we keep in mind the nature of what has been promised us in heaven and its greatness, then everything which we have here on earth becomes devalued for us.[11]

Contact with the absolute makes lesser things appear as they really are: of merely relative value.

Jesus' parable of the treasure hidden in a field gives the true sequence of events that mark our commitment to the kingdom of God: first discovery, then joy, and in the strength of that joy, detachment. This is true at the beginning of the journey and all the way through. Detachment presupposes a buoyant optimism following on discovery. It is not waiting naked in the cold, wondering what is supposed to happen next.

The kingdom of heaven is like a treasure hidden in a field. One who discovers that treasure hides it again and because of the joy which it brings, goes off and sells everything and purchases that field. (Matthew 13:44)

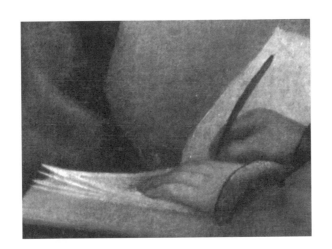

12

A STORY TO TELL

Among the many things we human beings require for survival and growth, one is not so generally recognized: the need I have to tell my story and have another person hear it. We each live through a unique complex of experiences and become what they make us. You can know nothing about me unless you understand what I have experienced and appreciate something of how I felt. If I do not have an opportunity to tell my story, I will feel distrustful of others and of the love they offer. If my experience is not brought into the open, it loses some of its reality, and will slowly slip beneath the threshold of my awareness. It will continue to shape my moods and reactions, but I will never know how or why. And others will not know what makes me act the way I do.

Speaking to men who were soldiers in the Second World War, I have been surprised how few really talk about what it felt like to live in peril of one's life. They chronicle events, tell yarns and express nostalgia for the "mateship" they experienced. They become sad, even tearful, when speaking of those who were killed. But rarely do they say anything of their own deep feelings. What happens when you take a fairly sensitive young man from among his loved ones and cast him into hell? They say it makes a man of him, but what happened to the boy? World War II was a trauma; Vietnam was unspeakably worse. Frequently those who came through the experience more or less physically intact experienced pressures as great as those whose lives were ravaged.

Being a soldier in wartime is a dramatic instance of what we all experience on the road to maturity. All experience similar horrors, even if there are no visible scars. Mostly we experience them alone. Our initiation into life is not much eased by myth-making or by rites of passage. Certainly no one goes through the experience with us. In a deep sense we travel alone.

We have companions, of course, and a few close friends. We may be fortunate to have as a spouse one who is all that we desire. Yet even then it is rare to experience such depth of communication that one feels known through and through. There are secrets, judiciously withheld or simply unmentioned. But what is not known cannot be loved; and what is not communicated to another feels unaccepted, rejected or even bad. What is not shared tends to divide. Sometimes love will perceive intuitively what cannot be framed in words. But often what is withheld acts as a barrier interrupting a relationship in ways neither party can understand, and causing pain to both. Even between close friends, or between husband and wife, there sometimes exists no opportunity to tell one's story.

Not that the *whole* story is ever told in this life. To do so would probably take longer than living it. Still, it is of great benefit to review the course of one's life with a few other persons, perceiving different highlights with different hearers. They draw from me complementary aspects of the whole.

Of course, we talk incessantly about what we have done, and maybe also how we feel. One knows people who keep talking about a few past events with an enthusiasm undimmed by the glazed expressions of those who endure it. Ordinary banter can be precious – it signals in code friendliness and acceptance. But when it concentrates on external reality, one begins to yearn for a deeper, more intimate level of communication. There are people so hungry for "a deep and meaningful conversation" that they become intrusive. Their solution is not the best, but they serve as a reminder of our shared need. Small talk becomes intolerable if one never has the opportunity to speak about more important things.

A few years ago, in a state of unimpeachable sobriety, I had a serious fall. Since I was abroad at the time, inevitably questions were asked on my return. For most, it was a matter of finding out the sequence of events – bones broken, blood, lacerations and black eyes, and so forth. These facts I retold, with a few imaginary flourishes. Only two or three close friends took the further step of inviting me to say how I felt during the whole affair: Was I in pain? Was I anxious about potential brain damage? What passed through my mind at that time? These were matters I was glad to talk about, but felt unable to do so in the context of a florid tale of blood and broken bones. Objectively the fall was a trivial incident, but for various reasons it was highly significant for me. As I talked to friends about its deeper aspects, the event became more real and its significance more potent.

It is my belief that in Western society we tend to underestimate the depth of human experience. We are more at ease dealing with objective facts and overt happenings than in opening toward what is beneath the surface. Undoubtedly this complicates life. One finds beneath a cheery, well-adjusted façade a vulnerability and a history of hurt. In the short term it is easier to interact by assuming a surface calm. Mostly we do not want to listen to pressures building up inside others; we prefer to hope they will muddle through, and (anyhow) we have enough worries on our own account. Perhaps the most necessary of all skills today is the timeless knack of being able to listen to others, allowing them to tell their story, knowing that telling it will ease their burden and help them become stronger. Personally, we should recognize how much it helps to speak to a few who are close to us about things that matter and about how we feel. Generally we are not looking to them for answers or solutions, simply for acceptance.

Among the deep and largely undiscussed aspects of our experience is prayer. Those whose prayer slips away are usually people without the opportunity to speak about their prayer experiences. So these times become unreal, and other priorities edge out prayer. Unless we think about our experiences of prayer and talk about them a little, we are unlikely to persevere. I am thinking here not so much of asking somebody to give one direction, but simply of recounting what has been one's experience. What I refer to could perhaps best be called "taking counsel."

The problem is to find someone with whom we feel comfortable in discoursing at such a level. Many will prefer to ease us away from what is irretrievably unique in our experience, back to common ground. Some cannot cope with the extent of our past hurt or present fragility. Few can gaze unblinkingly on our sinfulness or accept the strength of our moments of grace. We have to keep searching, inviting others to enter our inner space to the degree that it is possible. We may seek out a professional spiritual director, counsellor or psychoanalyst for certain areas of our life. But it is also possible that someone among our circle of acquaintances will provide the help we are looking for in our journey of prayer.

Keeping a journal can help – writing down from day to day, or as we feel inspired, whatever relates to our movement toward God. This helps us to externalize and give form to our experiences. It is also of assistance in getting our thoughts together so that when occasion offers to "tell my story" I am not left speechless. Having reflected already and written something, I will probably be able to communicate more accurately.

If one is fortunate enough to belong to a family, a group or a community where such things can be discussed with relative ease, one's degree of comfort with spiritual realities is likely to be considerably higher than otherwise. We may choose to review different aspects of our story with different persons. Some parts may be relatively public; others will remain confidential. Acceptance that we experience in one area may give us courage to face something else, long hidden. Sometimes another person may intervene delicately to suggest something we have been overlooking. And the knowledge of me that a confidant has will be a force toward my being authentic.

The official Church is so massive that one easily feels alienated from it. It does not always seem like friendly space. Its teaching on faith and morals may seem distant and aloof, unrelated to anything that I experience. The Church does not always present as being emphatic about personal development or human relations. It sometimes gives the impression of wanting to get a number of "good works" done through efficient bureaucratic and institutional means. It appears to suggest that if we want to participate in church life we have to fit into a slot. And that once there we will be very happy. But if we happen to be one of the increasing number of people for whom the Church seems to have no slot, what are we to do? Some attach themselves to a role or function within the organization and try to make do with an approximation. Others lose heart and leave the Church, regretful, but firmly believing themselves excluded.

If the Church could allow itself to be reduced to human scale, it could become a much more attractive focus for spiritual life. And in fact that is beginning. But it needs to happen more. In a more accessible church, the Scriptures and other spiritual patrimony of the ages would function as myth, revealing mysteries of the spirit to searchers, and unveiling our own hidden depths. Pastors would not be administrators of a written law, but people who understand when it is wise to insist and when it is better to bide one's time. Our brothers and our sisters would be known to us and we to them. Our prayer and mutual service, our dialogue, patience and fun would all be shared. Then our story could be told, because others would be ready to hear it.

This may seem as idealistic a picture of the Church as the one Saint Luke paints in the Acts of the Apostles. Idealistic means something toward which we aim; so I agree. I am not naïve however, in estimating the effort it would take to achieve. Nor do I underestimate the labors of so many who are attempting to create an accessible church. The ideal is worth being reminded of.

The Church is a natural home for all who wish to pray, and the more faithful the Church is to its charter the more effective it will be as a school of prayer and contemplation. There is no better accompaniment to growth in prayerfulness than a strong sacramental life and the constant proclaiming and hearing of the Gospel. The company of those who accept to rule their lives by Christ's teaching is a major advantage in the spiritual quest. The Church's outward movement toward aiding those who have less of anything can counterbalance any tendency to become too absorbed in one's own inner processes.

There is much wrong with the Church, but *we* are the Church. As we are purified by God's grace, we may begin to be more aware of just how much we have to contribute toward making the Church (or at least our part of it) a spiritual home for all who seek God. A place, too, where those who cannot yet grasp the ultimate meaning of their own experience may find counsel and understanding.

Apart from answering to my need to tell my story there are other benefits in taking counsel. It may be possible for the various functions I have in mind to be exercised by one person; more likely they will be spread over several. And different individuals do not require help to the same extent in all areas. I identify the following as the roles of a "soul-friend."

1. Initiation
2. Imparting a rule of life
3. Teaching about spiritual development
4. Accompaniment
5. Discernment
6. Re-initiation

1. Initiation

At a discernible point in many lives, religion ceases being an external, foreign reality and now is perceived as stemming from the heart. There is an awakening of the spiritual sense. Sometimes this occurs in solitude, but often there is a human intermediary. Up till this point the individual's spiritual quest, if indeed it was under way, seemed a matter of reason and will power. After initiation, it has access to more primal energies. The role of the initiator is to be a mirror in which the person in question sees his or her own spiritual potential and begins to glimpse a personal spiritual future. The fire may catch after a word, a glance or a touch. It may even occur in a dream. For the initiator, this is a moment of simple transparency in which God sees what he has made and declares it very good. For the person in question this may be a dramatic event, or a deep and sober one known only by its effects. This experience does not fade away but does recede somewhat into the background; if it is genuine, it continues to feed into one's prayer for years – perhaps for the rest of one's life. The soul-friend may have a role in helping translate this fundamental experience into the realm of prayer, even though it took place years previously. Whenever doubt and confusion appear, the memory of this moment will be a source of strength and guidance and an encouragement to begin again.

2. Imparting a rule of life

A soul-friend is a teacher of Gospel values and a transmitter of spiritual wisdom. Without relinquishing the demands of adult responsibility, I take counsel about the manner in which Christ's values find concrete expression in my life. Together we two draw up a flexible structure aimed at ensuring that the gift entrusted to me is not dissipated through easy-going ways, nor strait-jacketed by too firm a discipline. Those in religious life already have a rule, and many other people's lives are likewise determined by the demands of family and work. So the structure will deal with only those areas where there are options.

This rule of life is "imparted" by the soul-friend, not to give a new version of the Ten Commandments, but because in some sense one's "rule" should come from outside oneself. It should be imposed, as it were, by the Spirit. It should follow the state of one's prayer. If all is well, it is not the effect of the busy workings of the superego, but a practical expression of one's desire to build life outward, beginning from the heart. The soul-friend is one who reflects our spiritual disposition so the rule we adopt is authentic. To be obedient to it is to follow the heart, and to follow the heart is to move toward God.

3. Teaching spiritual development

While we live we grow, and as we grow we change. Responses that were appropriate at one stage do not necessarily fulfill our needs under different circumstances. Prolonged contact with a spiritual guide should mean more than noting one's day-by-day itinerary. One should gain a general idea of the journey as a whole. Nobody can give detailed directives for the years ahead, but no true guide would leave us in doubt about the likely consequences of continued spiritual growth. Apart from the regular fluctuations in life, which are best monitored as they occur, there are others that are more or less predictable. Some are normal human processes of maturation and decline – but the changes that accompany them are no less confusing for being universal. Others are more specifically concerned with spiritual growth and development in prayer. For all of these the soul-friend can prepare the way by anticipatory teaching. The "nights" Saint John of the Cross discusses are substantially more confusing and painful if one has no idea what is happening or why. Or how one might creatively respond. One does not give a novice in prayer detailed instructions about how to handle the "obscure night of the spirit," but as a person advances one tries to ensure that the strengths required for the next stage are beginning to emerge. One must foresee the next step, or the following phase may be one of regression. Unfortunately, it is possible for a director to invest so much energy identifying with progress as to be unable to cope with the reality of decline. So the individual is left stranded.

4. Accompaniment

Not everyone needs instruction, but we all appreciate having someone walk beside us on a long journey. It is a humble task, but crucially important – a matter of staying with the individual no matter where experience leads or what decisions the person makes. The one who accompanies will not always remain silent and may express opinions – or even recriminations – but always from within, never as an outsider. I need as soul-friend someone to whom I can freely submit whatever concerns me, knowing that the response given will be given truly. The other will not give in to fear of displeasing me by a negative answer. Nor will there be any attempt to manipulate me or inhibit my freedom. Instead, an honest reflection of my heart. And if I go astray, as frequently I do, I hope to be able to speak of my sin in all its ugliness, and in some way receive forgiveness and healing. I do not want to maintain a facade: surely the one who knows the best in me can bear to see a little of the worst.

No such relationship will be without its moments of discomfort. There will be times when I sense a distance is growing between us and misunderstandings seem just waiting to occur. In such a situation I may need to reflect a little, and perhaps initiate a dialogue on the state of the relationship. There are many possible reasons why a formerly creative relationship may be losing its punch. The other may be moving into a different space that makes it temporarily difficult to concentrate on attending to my needs. I may be bleeding my soul-friend for comfort and encouragement without ever reciprocating – or, more importantly, without looking to the other for challenge. Perhaps my friend feels uneasy about some elements in my behavior at present, but I am leaving no opening for comment. My soul-friend may withdraw somewhat if I am perceived as over-dependent or manipulative. The source of the difficulty may well be in me. It is worth staying with the relationship to discover why.

5. Discernment

By definition we are unaware of our blind spots. I do not know what proportion of my vision is blocked. I can never be sure whether what I see constitutes the whole of the reality confronting me or only a part; nor whether my sight is substantially or minimally impaired. I have to rely on what others tell me.

There are things in my life just as obstructive as a physical barrier. Others see them. It is no good their telling me about them if I am reluctant to listen, mistrusting both their vision and their motives for imparting the information. A soul-friend, however, I trust. With the aid of counsel I form a fuller picture of the reality that is myself – normally viewed only from the inside out. Even if I cannot actually see what the other perceives, I can act on trust. If I do not trust anyone, I will have to learn everything through painful experience. This involves being buffeted by life more than is necessary. The effect, since I am unsupported, may be to cause my spiritual life to shrink instead of helping it expand.

All the same, it can be difficult to accept another's perspective on one's actions, even when the other is a person we respect and trust. Even one who is a friend to my soul will often hold back until I give an opening for comment. The other's observation may be expressed diffidently so as not to arouse my hostility. In such a case I need to understand that the mildest reproof may be intended as the beginning of a dialogue. It should not be dismissed as an aimless aside.

A person who knows my personal history well and has some understanding of my character will often be very helpful in translating my spiritual experiences and aspirations into a style of life suitable for me – not merely imitative of the way others seem to live. One person's meat is another's poison. A course of action that attracts me may not necessarily be helpful to my growth in the way I hope. Those naturally quiet and withdrawn will often reinforce their natural tendency instead of supplementing it. They seek more silence and solitude, when what they need may be more social interaction. Extraverts may seek to be more communicative and more involved with others when what they really need is more depthing within themselves. We need not feel inferior because of what we are, but we need to do more than refine qualities in us that come naturally. We need challenge too. Here a soul-friend can help.

There are times of decision-making when I need help to perceive issues clearly and avoid blind spots, and especially to mobilize my spiritual resources. No one else should make the difficult decision for me, but one who serenely reflects to me my inner identity can make the choice clearer. There are other benefits as well: support, encouragement, continuity, information – and occasionally a well-administered rude awakening. In brief, a soul-friend may help us discern the meaning of what we have experienced and where we are being called.

Because it is generally solitary and interior, we often lack a precise idea of how our prayer is going. In normal times, one takes it for granted that all is going as well as can be expected. Sometimes, however, an event out of the ordinary happens that is worth discerning.

Some changes in prayer are developmental and occur almost predictably. Others come as a surprise. There are bodily reactions experienced during meditation that may or may not be connected with the prayer. Bodily changes, including sexual reactions, result from a variety of factors. Some who pray with hands outstretched, for example, experience an involuntary lifting of the arms – and it requires a slight effort to lower them. This muscular reaction, not unlike that seen among teenagers at rock concerts, is not particularly mystical. It is relatively neutral. It expresses beautifully the uplifting of the heart to God, and may indeed be experienced as prayer. But if it becomes the center of attention, God has been displaced and it is counter-productive. If accompanied by silly notions about one's elevated spiritual growth, it is certainly not to be encouraged. The same is to be said of visual impressions, whether abstract or with recognizable shapes, and words "heard." Such experiences are relatively common; they are neither signs of great prowess at prayer nor of psychosis. They are simply things that many people notice along the way. The one situation I consider almost always unhealthy is when an individual experiences a "message" *for others*; a good friend will generally treat evangelism of this kind with extreme caution.

I do not want to digress long regarding the possibility of going astray, but one warning is salutary. Religion has no monopoly on "nuts," but it certainly has its fair share. Some time ago a book called

Mind Games offered detailed instructions about how to produce all sorts of "experiences" in a group context, without any religious reference. In fact, altered states of consciousness, trances, accelerated mental processes, speaking in tongues and so forth can all be produced on a completely secular level by various techniques. So whatever experiences we have, there is no guarantee these come from God – no matter how extraordinary they seem. This is especially so when there is connivance on our part, such as becoming part of a group where such experiences are routine. It is possible to go astray, so it is a help to have someone who will be candid with us in commenting on our experiences – someone who constantly edges us away from preoccupation with subjectivity toward a more complete faith that expresses itself in contentment, with a very low level of conscious fireworks. Those who are transformed by prayer, instead of becoming spectacular mystics, become humble human beings. They are sustained from within: what they receive from elsewhere is considerably less important to them.

I shall add also a note about experiences of the demonic or, perhaps, the daimonic. Some people go through very vivid experiences of evil, whether as an outside force or as a stream of malignancy from inside. It is wise to talk over such experiences. Sometimes they are not what they seem. There are cases where the experiences seem related to a desire to go too far too quickly. In others, something pathological is at work. Sometimes what seems to be evil is really something good. In any event, it is worth taking counsel.

The best way to protect ourselves from delusive experiences is not to seek spiritual "highs" too ardently, but to be content with the ordinary Gospel way of fidelity and hope. This is well-illustrated in a story from the desert tradition. A monk was walking along an isolated road in the desert, completely intent on his prayers. A demon, seeing this, was vexed and sought to distract him. So the demon transformed himself into an angel of light and appeared at his side. The monk continued with his prayers. Eventually the "angel" drew attention to himself spectacularly. The monk's response was: "Go away! Can't you see I am saying my prayers?" The demon withdrew disappointed, knowing there was no way such a person could be led astray. There is strength in a stolid faith that refuses to be interested much in miracles, visions, apparitions or signs. A person genuinely united to God may feel such spectacular interventions as not only unnecessary but almost offensive. They can certainly be a cause of distraction and delusion.

6. Re-initiation

There are times in many people's lives when they believe everything is lost. So much energy has been expended on wrong directions or dissipated in self-indulgence that it requires a new and arduous beginning to turn toward God. For such persons there sometimes needs to be a positive intervention from a friend who can deftly cut away the rot that has accumulated and expose the heart. There is no question of denying the accumulated weight of sin, but of somehow demonstrating its puniness before the immensity of God's love. This cannot be conveyed through clichés. A dynamic intervention is required, one that can span the lost years and declare them finished, and can then reach the long-forgotten heart, in great need of being loved by God.

What the soul-friend does in such a case is rescue a person imprisoned in despair. Often sins have already been confessed and officially forgiven. What remains is a lingering sense that potential growth is now severely limited. Nothing could be further from the truth. But it may need another's intervention to re-awaken our dormant spiritual sense, and make us aware that without our desire for God, there is nothing of us as persons. A word, a touch, a look from another person may be enough to break down barriers that years have built.

The story of the soul is an important and often neglected part of our history. It is a great gift from God to have access at different stages of our development to people with whom we can share some episodes. If there is one person to whom we can entrust our experience, who is qualified in understanding and in feeling to serve as friend to our soul, we are doubly blessed. One cannot, however, wait forever in the hope that the ideal person will materialize. One may need to risk something with a few of one's closer associates, knowing that such communication could establish a climate of greater mutual trust from which to work toward the ideal. I do not underestimate the risk. But sometimes one must be prepared to take the initiative to improve a situation, rather than merely hope.

It is hard to believe that in heaven our whole story will be naked and exposed to all, and that somehow the totality of our experiences will then seem a unity – not composed of good and bad, but of elements each contributing their own unique share to the final glory. "For them that love God all things work together unto good" (Romans 8:28). We cannot now see it. At best, our lives appear battlegrounds for opposing forces. We are aware of failures and sins. One who sees with the eye of God perceives more. In the context of the whole there is much beauty – even in the things we cannot completely love. A soul-friend, in accepting our story, accepts us. There is a moment of transparency where one begins to understand one's lovableness in God's eyes. From that point, there can be no looking back.

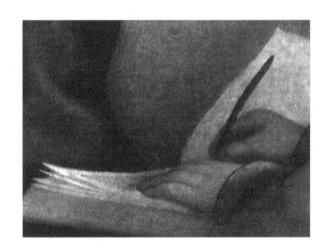

13

THE CROSS OF
JESUS CHRIST

Our journey toward the Father is not made possible by anything we are or anything we do. It is entirely gift. By persevering in prayer one becomes strongly aware that prayer exceeds human capabilities. Much effort is involved in being faithful to prayer, but nothing we can do directly causes it to emerge.

Prayer is the work of the Holy Spirit. Even the measures we take to ensure our mind is unencumbered and to find the time for God come from the Spirit's action. "God is at work in us both to will and to accomplish" (Philippians 2:13). Our task is to step aside and allow the Lord to get on with it. We do not mastermind our prayer, but aim to be attentive to the Spirit's promptings through conscience, through our contact with the Scriptures, through those we encounter at the level of the spirit and through the church. We truly pray in the Spirit when we are so convinced of our resourcelessness that we are prepared to be empty – even though prolonged experience of this emptiness is profoundly painful.

In this emptiness we are not alone. Jesus Christ is our companion. The Word of God emptied himself to become one of us (Philippians 2:7). He who was from all eternity toward-God put on human nature in all its awayness-from-God. In the incarnation the Word embraced the human experience of being far from the Father: far by virtue of the limited extent of human receptivity, with life scattered over a series of mutually exclusive moments; far by subjecting himself to the slow rhythms of unfolding human development; and, finally, by sin, even though there was no personal sin – he was like unto us "in all things *except sin*" (Hebrews 4:15). The experience of being away-from-the-Father reached its greatest depth on Calvary when, as a prelude to being assumed into God, Jesus cried out, "O my God, my God, why have you abandoned me?" (Mark 15:34).

Jesus took upon himself all the experience of our estrangement from God. He is the Lamb of God who *bears* (the double meaning is present in the Greek text and in the Latin liturgy) the sin of the world (see John 1:29). He assumed our sinfulness. In fact Saint Paul goes further: "For our sake, God made sin the one who was without sin, so that in him we might become the righteousness of God" (2 Corinthians 5:21). In solidarity with sinful humanity, Jesus experienced all the horror of separation from the Father, so that he could show us the way to return.

How does all of this relate to prayer? When I pray, I become conscious of my personal need for God, and mysteriously aware too, that although my own situation is the immediate stimulus of prayer, I pray with the voice of all humanity. I express in myself the totality of human need for God. Or perhaps better, Christ prays within wounded humanity. From the midst of the experience of fragility and vulnerability, Christ continues to make intercession (see Hebrews 7:25). As I pray Christ is, through the Spirit, interior to my prayer: when I plead for mercy, it is with Christ as intermediary and advocate with the Father (see 1 John 2:1).

Parallel with my prayer is sacramental life – which initiates the process whereby Christ lives through me. By baptism I come to share his status as one begotten of the Father, and become myself "a sharer in the divine nature" (2 Peter 1:4). Throughout the stages of my life, Christ is with me and in me as a power of transformation and "the hope of glory" (Colossians 1:27). The new life of Christ's resurrection acts on me, moving me toward that ultimate beauty and perfect fulfillment we name in the Creed: "the resurrection of the body and life everlasting."

All this is true. However, Christ's way to glory was through the cross. Children of the resurrection though we are, we reach this goal only through the mystery of Christ's death. In a sense Christ must die within us to be raised to a newness of life. This aspect of spiritual living is a scandal and a folly to those who do not have the mind of Christ (see 1 Corinthians 1:23). Christ dies within us because of sin: by internalizing the rejection of others and by our own acts of rejection we turn from God and move to terminate the life of Christ in us. This amounts to the ultimate act of self-destruction – destroying what alone can lead us to beauty and happiness.

We do not understand sin, because there is nothing to understand. Sin is a denial and rejection of meaning, a turning away from what is good, true and beautiful. Its malice consists precisely in its perverse preference for non-being over being, for non-reality over reality. Sin is the ultimately absurd human act. We can analyze what leads up to it and predict its consequences, but we never understand what makes a human will choose to turn away from its proper object. By sin we deny God; we deny Christ; in the last analysis we deny ourselves. We twist our nature out of shape.

Because one cannot understand sin, one may be tempted to doubt its reality. Or call it relatively harmless mischief – like violating a code of obligations intended for somebody much better than I am. Humiliated by my inability to will sin away, I may try to imagine it away, or to rationalize my situation. But denial merely renders its destructive effects invisible to me; this is blindness to danger, not freedom. We make no progress by forgetting sin and concentrating on "positive realities" – because progress is a matter of a deeper apprehension of truth. Spiritual growth is hastened considerably by our becoming more aware of the *reality* of sin in our life. This must cause grief, because delusions and complacency will be shattered. Completing the process will involve long labor, under grace – a lifetime spent repairing damage and minimizing future harm.

In some mysterious way we attain a depth of experience of God only by being exposed to our sinfulness, as individuals and as members of a sinful race. Moreover, awareness of sin serves as a generator of prayer. As Saint Augustine remarked, "Because we are human we are also weak; because we are weak, we pray."[1] To deny one's proneness to evil is ultimately to deny one's humanity. And though we cannot understand why we need to know our sinfulness before we really learn to pray, experience shows this is so.

Unfortunately we do not learn about sinfulness from a heavenly messenger. Nor is it like the result of a personality test. We learn of our sinfulness when we are tempted. Temptation is more than awareness of alternative options: I am not tempted to genocide if I lack the means; I am not tempted to computer fraud if I am insufficiently skilled. These are *not* temptations. A real temptation involves a combination of elements: an external assault with the collusion of a fifth column within. It needs at least a 65 percent chance of success; otherwise inertia intervenes and the status quo prevails. Jesus Christ was tempted but was never defeated (Hebrews 4:15). When I am tempted sin often results, although sometimes the outcome is delayed by a token resistance. This is the sordid reality of my life. My tendency in prayer is then to try to put my sin behind me. Acknowledging only that it was an interruption in our relationship, I want to forget it when I come before God. This is a mistake. It is like hiding one's symptoms from a physician. To go to prayer aware of the shabbiness of my life is a great blessing. I can approach God as the great Healer of life's wounds, reveal myself in truth, and receive help. If I avoid the issue by keeping up a barrage of words and holy thoughts, I end up exhausted – and God is rendered powerless by my reluctance to be honest. My failures, I must learn, do not separate me from God. What causes the breach is an unwillingness to bring my failures into God's presence. The greater failure is not realizing that God's attitude to my sin is pity, not blame.

Here the teaching of Julian of Norwich is splendid:

> After this [God] allows us to fall harder and more grievously than ever we did before – as it seems to us. And then we think (because we are not all wise) that what we had begun has come to nothing. But it is not so. It is necessary for us to fall and it is necessary for us to see it. For if we did not fall we should not know how feeble and wretched we are on our own, nor should we know so fully the marvelous love of our Maker.
>
> For, in truth, we shall see in heaven for all eternity that though we have grievously sinned in this life, we were never hurt in God's love, nor were we ever of less value in God's sight. This falling is a test by which we shall have a high and marvelous knowing of love in God for ever. That love is hard and marvelous that cannot and will not be broken for [our] trespasses.[2]

By falling we have the chance to plumb the mysteries of the divine mercy. Indeed our sin is a happy fault, as the deacon sings during the Easter vigil: *O felix culpa!* But this is sin admitted, accepted and confessed, not sin hidden, denied and forced underground. God does not forgive grudgingly; showing mercy is an act continuous with the love in which we were created. Julian has her own way of describing God's mercy:

> I see that mercy is a sweet, gracious working in love, mingled with plenteous pity. Mercy works by preserving us and mercy works by turning all things to our good. In love, mercy allows us to fail somewhat, and in failing we fall, and in falling we die. For death is inevitable since we lack the sight and experience of God who is

[the source] of our life. Our failing is full of fear; our falling
marked by sin and our dying is sorrowful. Yet, in all this, the sweet
eye of pity never departs from us and the working of mercy never
ceases.[3]

In a manner beyond our comprehension, Christ must die within us
and so come to the splendor of the resurrection. We feel his death
because with each sin something of us dies also. Each denial of life
reduces one's general level of vitality. As the years accumulate so too
can a massive weight of guilt stemming from wrong choices, unwise
preferences and momentary gratifications. We have put to death the
life of Christ within us. If we are sensible we will be soberly aware of
this – not frantically or extravagantly guilty but quietly and
realistically recognizing our responsibility.

"Yet, in all this, the sweet eye of pity never departs from us and
the working of mercy never ceases." We have not chosen God, we
ourselves have been chosen; we have rejected God, we have not been
rejected. Though the weight of sin exercises its inhibiting influence
over us, astonishingly God continues to love us. And the paradoxical
sign that love is at work is that we glimpse the extent to which we
have damaged ourselves. When we become aware of our actual state,
whether suddenly or by a gradual process, this is not because we have
become worse (though sometimes it is the last straw that breaks
through our resistance) but because we now recognize what was
holding us back. Though one is ashamed of actions that brought this
sinful tendency into the open, in fact it would have exercised its
influence whether it was visible or invisible. Now that we know about
it, we can begin to change, with God's help. As Saint Augustine
explains:

> It is already a gift of the Holy Spirit that what you have done is
> displeasing to you. Sins please the unclean spirit and displease the
> Holy Spirit. Although it is pardon that you are pleading for, still,
> because the evil that you have committed is a source of displeasure
> to you, you become one with God. For what displeases you also
> displeases him. Now the two of you are contending against your
> fever: you and the physician. The confession and punishment of
> sin are not possible for a human being unaided, so when one is
> angry with oneself, then this does not take place without the gift
> of the Holy Spirit.[4]

Knowledge of our sinfulness, then, is the first stage in our restoration. In exposing our resourcelessness, God draws us toward prayer, and so toward a boundless outpouring of mercy.

I believe one of the most intense experiences of suffering a Christian can endure is not persecution, nor the difficulty of proclaiming the Gospel to an unbelieving world, nor illness and pain – not even grief. Nowhere does one experience the anguish of Christ's cross so keenly as in realizing the extent to which one has fallen under the power of sin. Other trials are in some sense external; overcoming them requires fortitude, patience and the power to endure. But when the will itself is permeated with malice, the situation is dire – not unlike AIDS. Infection can be fought while the immune system is operating. But when the body's defenses are radically weakened, death can follow from any infection that happens along. Radical sinfulness leaves us similarly resourceless in the face of temptation We experience an incapacity to fight sin. Our ability to resist evil has been subverted.

To those who have made the following of Christ their first priority in life, this discovery comes as a severe shock. It is an occasion of dread, appearing to indicate that one's direction in life is hopeless: "Then we think ... that what we had begun has come to nothing." The fact that one cannot discover any reason why the will is so irremediably perverse deepens one's sense of alarm and erodes confidence. If we knew the cause of our decline, we might try to reverse the situation. But we cannot identify what in us has caused the blindness, weakness and malice. It is truly a mystery.

It is, I believe, this discovery of our own radical powerlessness for good and potential for evil that causes us to be identified with the crucified Christ. The details vary for each individual: they may concern the governance of one's own life, bringing up one's family or one's work for the Church. Instead of being filled with the power of the Spirit we find ourselves empty and resourceless, victims of our own weaknesses and, quite possibly, the objects of others' disapproval. Generally one's first solution is to work harder, trying to demonstrate competence. The situation deteriorates further. What we need to do is take the powerlessness as a basic premise, and use this as a fulcrum to lift our hearts in prayer toward God.

Sometimes progress requires doing the exact opposite of what seems appropriate. At the beginning the solution most people bring to any prayer problem is to try harder. As time goes on, we meet resistance that does not yield to willpower. In a sense, we have to try less – and certainly change tactics. When things go wrong, working frantically to prove there is no underlying cause is ineffectual, or worse. The problem must be faced squarely, with no cover-up. This means having the courage to see through the problem to our own resourcelessness – see it, but also feel it. Anything that disguises our inner poverty is to be avoided. Facile "solutions" only postpone the agony. The way forward is to look honestly at the disaster, accept responsibility for it and then begin to redefine oneself and one's relationship with God in terms of the experience. Easily said, very painful to accomplish. The old image of self has to die so that a more authentic self can be born. The old self has to die, not only in its undesirable features, but in some of the very components we have previously identified as Christ's life within us.

In this way we grow up, leaving behind the things of childhood and abandoning ourselves to the divine pedagogy. But not without anguish. And sometimes the process of being broken open inside begins to show on the surface. A person well regarded by others now finds, with alarm, that the rubbish accumulated within begins to become visible. One may even experience rejection because of it. A wise observer might say that what looks like regression is in fact putting aside illusory progress and touching the truth. But wise observers are rare. As far as most people are concerned we are going through a bad stage, perhaps even going into terminal decline. But the grain of wheat has germinated: it has broken through the hard husk enclosing its soul and is in process of generating rich and radiant life. To the person in question it feels like dissolution.

It is hard to see that one's previous life, harmless and pious as it was, has to be grown out of. Growth is impossible without our being troubled – and the troubles themselves have an active role in detaching us from what is of relative value and directing us toward God. As Augustine says of God:

> You fill all things with troubles so that human beings may, in time of trouble, have recourse to you instead of being seduced by delights and false security ... Trouble is active so that the vessel which is full of evil may be emptied in order that it may be filled with grace.[5]

We feel the pain and resist it; yet as God's work advances, we sense that there is a rightness about it. There is no question of God making us pay for our past sins. The wrenching is caused by efforts to turn the ship around. This is not blind suffering, but somehow related to what we have made of ourselves. It is a great advance to be able to see some of life's suffering as helping offset our estrangement from God – much of it the result of seeking comfort and pleasure. Speaking of King David's repentance, Augustine notes that this episode enabled David to bear his later troubles more stoutly, seeing that he believed that whatever he received was less than his crimes merited.

> He walked in sorrow, troubled and humiliated. And he was so subject to God that he confessed that all that God did was just and that there was nothing that he himself had to suffer which was unfair. Thus he pleased God for his heart was upright. He acknowledged his fault, he embraced his penalty, for the glory he sought was not his own.[6]

If one accepts that our troubles fall within the providence of God, one is more likely to see them as potentially beneficial, and not necessarily destructive. In the case of others, it is easier to see that hard times have frequently been turned to good account in the long run – not that we ever callously close our hearts to those in difficulty and say, "It is all for the best." But because suffering is part of human experience, we need to think more about rendering it creative than about avoiding it. Pain can be reduced and should be. But it cannot be totally eliminated. Whether we suffer much or little the philosophic questions remain. Why suffering? Why me? These become especially acute when we have been instrumental in laying the foundations for our own distress.

Through our troubles we can enter a level of human truth not accessible by any other means. When we identify with Christ crucified, our spiritual life takes on reality and solidity. Strangely, by facing the worst in ourselves we can begin to perceive the glimmer of a hope that is unshakable. Renouncing the appearance of virtue and the illusion of innocence is a great advance. Confessing our sinfulness, without dissimulation or exaggeration, comes as a great relief. Somehow it confers an awareness that from the depths of our being we desire God. We begin to experience such love for God that we take no pleasure in our virtue – and are not surprised by our vice. We seem to move beyond morality into the sphere of a more personal orientation toward God.

Through suffering, one comes to depend less on external things for satisfaction, and to confront inward reality more squarely. From here it is a small step toward God. As Augustine says to his congregation:

> You have gone astray by your wandering abroad. Return! But to where? To the Lord. It is time: first return to your heart, for you have been an exile from yourself in wandering abroad. How can you hope to seek your Maker when you do not know yourself. Return, return to your heart ... Christ lives within the human being, there you are renewed in the image of God. In his image, recognize its author.[7]

As noted earlier, we come to know God by understanding the work taking place within us – creation, restoration and the forgiveness of our sins. God's action in our hearts is a revelation.

"Confidence is learned by experience."[8] We are never really sure unless we have tried something for ourselves. This is true of the mercy of God. Sureness about forgiveness comes from having one's sins forgiven. This is a point Jesus himself made. Only one who has had many sins forgiven can love deeply (see Luke 7:47). Even if we seem through malice to have ended Christ's life within us, there is still scope for mercy. We can always pray. We are certainly not excluded from the prayer of the tax-collector (Luke 18:13); nor from the Our Father, which asks forgiveness of sins, protection from temptation and deliverance from the power of the evil one (Matthew 6:12–13). Even the Hail Mary includes the clause, "Pray for us sinners." There is no evidence at all in Christian tradition that sin disqualifies us from prayer.

Surprisingly, sin does not exclude us even from the highest states of prayer. *The Cloud of Unknowing* is clear about this:

> See that no one think it presumption – even though the most wretched sinner of this life – to dare to proffer a meek stirring of love to God, secretly assailing the cloud of unknowing that blocks the way to God. This for one who feels attracted to that life which is called contemplative – with the assent of counsel and conscience.[9]

Sin is negated by love, and prayer is the expression of love. The awareness of sin does not drive out prayer, but renders it imperative. By praying we give scope to love. To the extent that we are controlled by love, God reigns supreme and sin's tyranny is voided.

Saint Bernard of Clairvaux is emphatic about this. For him, our capacity to enter the closest loving union with God is grounded in our nature; it can never be lost. No matter what troubles one makes for oneself, there are always grounds to hope for pardon – even grounds for a boisterous confidence about attaining the ultimate.

> It is my teaching that every soul
> although burdened with sins,
> although caught in a trap,
> although a captive in exile,
> although imprisoned in its body,
> although clinging to the mud and stuck in the mire,
> although afflicted with sorrows,
>   made anxious by many worries
>   and unsettled by suspicions,
> although it is a traveller in a hostile land
>   and thus, as the Prophet says,
>   soiled by contact with the dead
>   and reckoned with those in hell,
> this is what I say:
> that although a soul is so condemned and so desperate,
> nevertheless it is my teaching that
> such a soul is able to find *within itself*
> not only a source of relief in the hope of pardon
>   so that it may hopefully seek mercy,
> but also it will find a *source of boldness*
> so that it may desire marriage with the Word,
> not fearing to enter into a treaty of friendship with God
> nor being timid about taking up the yoke of love
>   from him who is the King of angels.
> *For what cannot safely be dared*
> *when the soul sees itself*
> *as God's excellent image*
> *and distinguished likeness?* [10]

Nothing in this life can put us outside the range of God's mercy.

Distress is our experience as Christ dies within us. We feel isolated in our resourcelessness. Yet we are sustained by the grace of God and by the mysterious presence of the whole company of God's people. There is enough flotation in the communion of saints to keep us from sinking totally – though we are unable to save ourselves. This is reflected in the way the fourth Evangelist describes Christ's own death: At the cross of Jesus there stood Mary his mother, the faithful women and the unnamed "disciple whom Jesus loved" (John 19:25–26). When the worst happens, one may well feel that the only factor that keeps us from going over the edge is the unseen accompaniment of "a great cloud of witnesses" (Hebrews 12:1) – those gone before who now support us. We may find ourselves specially aware of the maternal presence of Mary, mother of Jesus and of the Church.

Christ dies within us – to be raised in newness of life. Prayer will carry us far into the paschal mystery, though there will be times when we believe ourselves utterly alienated from any spiritual process. Everything in us that is hostile to God must be uncovered, and its bitterness tasted, before we can eliminate it. We will begin to wonder whether anything will survive such radical purgation. All that remains, in fact, will be what God has created and restored. Of our own unaided work and achievements there will be nothing. Our glory is to be transparent. If the face of God shines through us, we will be perfect in both beauty and happiness. Efforts to leave our mark result only in obscuring that radiance.

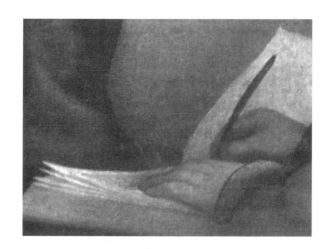

14

CONTEMPLATION

As Christians we are baptized into the death of Jesus Christ. This is not to say that we become thereby liable to death. Death is the common destiny of the human family. What our baptism brings us is not further death but the transformation of death into a doorway to eternal life. Christians are not immune from diminishment and dying, but through their identification with Christ these disabling experiences lose their capacity to harm us permanently (1 Corinthians 15:55). It is the paradox of Christianity that death becomes the means to life.

This is not to say that we cease to fear our own deaths or feel no grief at the deaths of those we love. The life-giving properties of death are not perceived directly any more than the health-restoring power of a bitter medicine. Some people have strong "intimations of immortality," an intuitive assurance of their personal survival; for others there is more trepidation. But, for all of us, death remains an awesome mystery and, as usual, we are uncomfortable with anything we do not fully understand. We learn about the other side of death from our faith. All that we have discovered in our lifelong encounter with God makes us trust that, in the end, all will go well with us. We are also buoyed up by the clear teaching of the New Testament and the witness of the Church. Perhaps the "near death experiences" recounted by some render us more receptive of the possibility of an afterlife. Fundamentally, however, our hope of eternal life is the result of our acceptance of the Gospel.

We are called to share not only the death of Jesus but his continuing life – the power of ongoing love that draws him simultaneously toward the Father and also toward humanity. The Resurrection is not simply an event that took place on Easter Sunday. It is a continuing state. Jesus lives. The same is true of that other aspect of the paschal mystery to which we pay less heed – the Ascension.

The Ascension is often presented as the final scene in the earthly career of Jesus. After the Resurrection he bids farewell to his disciples and disappears from this earthly stage, never to be seen again. In this sense the Gospel account has inspired many religious painters. Jesus rises up into the clouds. Many questions are left unanswered. The Gospel simply tells us he went up into the sky.

It is important that we view the mystery of Christ's Ascension less like a pantomime event these popular presentations suggest. To do this we have to rethink the occurrence with more sober imagery. This means tracking back to a few fundamental concepts.

When the second Person of the Trinity became human, what happened? Saint John tells us that "the Word became flesh" (John 1:14). What this means is that the Word who exists eternally beyond space and time became subject to spatio-temporal limitation. The fullness of the godhead began to dwell in a human body, located in only one place and thereby absent from every other; present to only one moment at a time and distant from all other moments. The Word became flesh as a first-century Palestinian male who knew nothing about Australia, space travel or the theory of relativity. "Flesh" signifies a mode of presence that is strictly localized in space and time, that is, in fact, more absence than presence. It is a very fragmented form of existence, because it is dispersed into a few distinct times and places; in moving to a new zone of life we necessarily leave behind what had become familiar. Human life is a ceaseless cycle of beginnings and endings. Even more than that, our being is filtered and changed by the zone we inhabit. We are not only localized, we are inculturated. Because we belong to a particular area of space-time, we inherit a specific mind-set with its own beliefs and values that form our character and mediate our personality. To choose one historical moment is not only to select the stage on which we play, it also determines the concrete character who is the subject of our actions.

When we say that the Word became contingent on spatio-temporal factors and thereby limited, we imply that the humanity of Jesus Christ was directly accessible only to those who coincided with him in space, time and culture. Caesar Augustus never knew Christ, though he was a contemporary – nor did Abraham, though he traversed the same countryside. When certain Greeks wanted to speak with Jesus they had to rely on an intermediary (John 12:20–22). Personal contact was limited to those who were able to get in touch with the physical reality of his body and communicate with him. This is why we say that the revelation of God in Jesus Christ was essentially a historical reality. For us to make contact with Jesus and his teaching we have to rely on the chain of tradition which links us with those who had firsthand experience of the man himself. Hence the role of the Church in bringing us the good news through the proclamation of the Scriptures and the witness of believing generations.

This "external" promulgation of the Gospel is complemented by the workings of the Holy Spirit at a more internal level. The fact that we accept the outward proclamation as true is possible only because we have already been initiated interiorly into the Mystery described in these outward forms. Jesus says, "No one can come to me unless drawn by the Father who sent me" (John 6:44). It is this inward anointing by the Holy One (1 John 2:20) that powers our faith. In some mysterious way there is a harmony between our deepest layer of experience and the content of the Church's proclamation.

It seems that in the heart of every believer there is an intimate contact with the Word. Usually this is at a preconscious level. We ourselves are scarcely aware of what drives us. Christians are made so, not because of some form of social pressure or neurosis. We have been touched by Christ at the center of our being, and throughout our lives we are unconsciously seeking to exchange this subtle contact for a full-blown relationship.

Let us return to the mystery of the Ascension. What does it mean? It means that the humanity of Jesus Christ which, during his career in Palestine, was radically restricted in terms of spatio-temporal presence now becomes universally accessible. In the paschal mystery the humanity of Jesus Christ remains, but it is a humanity no longer localized at specific points in space and time. It is a humanity now present at *all points* in the spatio-temporal continuum. The Ascension is not an occasion for "good-bye"; if anything, it is a time for "welcome." It is a departure from this earthly sphere only in the sense that it involves transcending those limitations that constitute us as historical beings. By reason of the Incarnation, the Word became part of human history. In the state resulting from his Resurrection and Ascension this presence continues without restriction. The Word-become-flesh not only sits at the right hand of the Father; he continues to be with his disciples on earth. The final words attributed to Jesus in the Gospel of Matthew are precisely a promise of permanent presence: "Behold I am with you through all days until the consummation of the age" (Matthew 28:20).

As far as concerns our practice of prayer it can be said that it is this cosmic presence of Christ that grounds its possibility. At the heart of prayer is person-to-person contact with the living Lord. Prayer is not historical reconstruction of Gospel scenes, nor an imaginary conversation with an unseen party named "God"; it is not metaphysical speculation, nor is it the utter blankness of evacuated consciousness. Prayer is interpersonal union with the tri-personal God: Father, Son and Holy Spirit. It is a matter of becoming aware of a God who is already close to us in Christ.

If we accept that such theological teaching has a basis in fact, then we may wonder why this all-pervading presence is not immediately evident to us. When Nikita Khrushchev told the first astronauts to keep an eye peeled for God while they were up there, I presume he was joking. We don't expect to see God with our bodily eyes – simply because we can sense only what is spatio-temporally limited. We can't see God by some sort of intellectual vision, because cognition depends on a sensory infrastructure which cannot contain divinity. It is only at the level of spirit that God is visible. For us to see God we have to leave behind the world of sense, enter the region of unknowing and allow the Holy Spirit to be our guide. "If we have known Christ Jesus according to the flesh, then we know him thus no longer" (2 Corinthians 5:16).

This is why prayer is often described in terms of silence and darkness. It is dark because at the level of sense or understanding there is nothing to see; nothing to feel or encompass with our wills. Perhaps there is nothing to experience, in the ordinary meaning of the word. Communion with God could be described as *meta-experiential*: it is something that transcends anything else we do or suffer. This is not the same as saying that it is unreal. It belongs to a different order of reality. The contemplative act requires of its nature a refined sensibility. That is why every tradition of prayer includes on its menu a solid diet of discipline, asceticism, purification and self-control. To bring ourselves to the point where we can be responsive to the Spirit's leading and allow ourselves to be drawn toward God, a lot of the dross of selfishness must first be burnt away. When much is happening at the level of consciousness, we are too easily attracted away from the dense silence of God. To be content with minimal experience at a level of feeling and consciousness is a prerequisite to being initiated into the more subtle states that accompany a deepening experience of God present.

If it is true that we were made for God, if baptism renders us participant in the very nature of God, then contemplation brings to fulfillment the promise contained in these earlier gifts. It is not something reserved to an elite, but a promise offered to all. In this earthly condition our potential for experiencing the reality of communion with God is limited by our subjective dispositions and by external factors. As life goes on, however, we often find that our problems sort themselves out, with God's grace, and it becomes more feasible for us to live in inner harmony. As this happens – and as our environment permits – we begin to catch glimpses of the reality of God's presence, even in situations from which we had thought God would be absent. Such momentary encounters often contain challenge as well as consolation. If we respond creatively and do not close the door, then God may begin to visit us more frequently.

These graced moments of divine intimacy can never be engineered by us; there is always something unpredictable and even whimsical about them. They do not bring us any overt advantage: new ideas or spectacular vistas. In fact, the deeper the experience, the less likely it will be to have obvious fringe benefits. Even our morals will remain unimproved in the short term. Nevertheless an invisible bonding takes place that slowly cements the human will with that of God. In time this becomes evident in a burgeoning of love; but such a result is not immediate.

The first effect of such an experience is to feel abashed. Without knowing it we may have moved beyond the zone where ordinary rules apply. To ourselves we seem beyond the pale; those whom we consult may be unable to help. If they have no experience of it, they had better not try. What is beyond human control is also outside our capacity to understand. What is beyond experience cannot be interpreted and explained in normal language. We have to learn to be content with unknowing. We are passive at this moment: God is the one who acts. In the last analysis, we have simply to assent to be led blindly, but we give this trust lovingly and lightly. It cannot be the grudging compliance of a slave.

Granted the essential human passivity inherent in divine initiative and action, the most we can do is to learn the art of sitting quietly and waiting for the salvation of the Lord (see Lamentations 3:26). This sounds easy, but it involves the renunciation of all efforts to control our own destiny, every tendency to cling to our grisly catalog of grievances and our arrogant desire to succeed in our own right. We sit in silence and wait for the coming of God.

The silence into which we are called is not blankness. Progressively it seems hostile. Just as the desert was traditionally seen not as the spot for a quiet retreat, but a howling wilderness in which demons lived, so God calls us not to rest but to a greater fidelity to truth. This closer attachment to ultimate reality is not possible unless we learn to abandon all that is unreal, untrue and not authentic in our lives. There is a hard-edged quality about the demands of this moment that does not yield to our usual tactics of evasion. We cannot satisfy them by rewriting our press releases, telling our story in a different way, highlighting different aspects of our past to accommodate new expectations. God is truth and if we are to encounter God at the level of spirit we have to leave behind our familiar falsehoods and live by a new law. This is not a matter of shedding obligations and reprogramming our lives. The regime of the Spirit is materially scarcely different from that previously given us from outside. Its special characteristic is that it derives its energies from within not from hope of rewards or the fear of sanctions. It is the law of freedom.

No matter how much we like the word "freedom" the reality can be a little frightening. "Freedom is just another word for nothing left to lose." To become free we have to allow all binding attachments to be loosed. Freedom is nakedness, according to the ancient maxim, "Naked to follow the naked Christ." For much of our life the rigor of this precept is waived. At a certain point, however, we are suddenly confronted with its exigency. We have lost much, we have been the victims of destructiveness, and now we are called freely to give up the little that remains. It seems so unreasonable. And yet unless we neutralize our paltry possessiveness we will be left in limbo indefinitely. We may ruefully discover that it is easier to be generous in a time of abundance than to give what seems to be our last, pitiable resource. But it is precisely this final and radical act of trust that God requires of us at this time.

In our putting aside of all other hopes we learn to live by a hope that seems hopeless. We no longer have the fig leaves of pretense to cover our native indigence and somehow we are relieved that we no longer have to keep up appearances. At this point we begin to know what it is to be "poor in spirit." Although this involves nothing less than seeing ourselves as God sees us, we resist the process mightily. As delusions drop off, we become more violently assailed by truth. So it appears. The truth seems mostly bad news. We begin to perceive something of the ugliness and compromise that have disfigured most of our past deeds and still hang around us like a bad smell. Yet, unwelcome though this hard truth be, there is comfort here. Our feet are on the ground. We are touching bottom. Mysteriously, just as God's passion for us is not diminished by our sinfulness, so this new vision of our need for God makes us share a little of God's unconditional love for us. What a surprise! The more we see the unwelcome truth about ourselves through God's eyes, the more accepting we become of our own reality. Our love and self-esteem increase because, now, even our self-love is shaped by God.

There is a fire that burns beneath these gray ashes that are all that remains of human achievement. Beneath the dullness there is an emergent passion. The dim light is not twilight but dawn. To have penetrated to the heart and to have found freedom there, does not offer much consolation at the level of emotion or intellect, but it carries its own subtle legitimation. We no longer feel inclined to go back to mental fireworks or powerful experiences, because somehow they have lost their appeal. They can be left aside as means that have served their purpose and are no longer needed. As Thomas Merton wrote in his last book:

> Contemplative prayer is, in a way, simply the preference for the desert, for emptiness, for poverty. One has begun to know the meaning of contemplation when he [sic] intuitively and spontaneously seeks the dark and unknown path of aridity in preference to every other way. The contemplative is one who would rather not know than know. Rather not enjoy than enjoy. Rather not have *proof* that God loves him.[1]

Far from being a "problem" in prayer such aridity – given the presence of other authenticating signs – can be the entrance into an interior state that progressively transforms the whole person. Especially in the early phases of it, there is a certain malaise, a nostalgia for the past and a desire to "fix things" – even though one dimly senses that nothing is broken. This is a crucial point when a decision has to be taken concerning who is in charge. If it is to be God, then back off. Let God act.

At times one may have experiences that are a little esoteric. There may be moments of intense absorption when one seems to disappear and return without knowing exactly where one has been. At times the body may join unbidden in the dance of prayer or there may be some overflowing into one's inner sensibility. Other effects may be more habitual such as a certain detachment from what are experienced as the trivialities of daily life, church politics or theology. Having touched the essential, be it ever so briefly, one's taste for the banal is permanently damaged.

Mostly, however, it is a matter of persevering with the low-impact landscape of quiet prayer and following our ordinary, obscure and laborious round. Perhaps we are conscious of an elusive awareness that backgrounds our activities like a half-remembered melody. One moment it is there; the next it flits away like a shy little bird that knows we are looking at it. The most immediate demand is that we do not lose faith in God's leading of us. We are not to curtail our devotion because it seems to accomplish nothing. As *The Cloud of Unknowing* puts it in a text quoted earlier, "Keep on doing this nothing." This is the ultimate detachment to which we are called, that we give ourselves to "nothing" in preference to every other possibility. It takes grit. Thus, Julian of Norwich places this exhortation in the mouth of Christ:

> Pray with your whole being even though you think that it has no savor for you. For such prayer is very profitable even though you feel nothing. Pray with your whole being, though you feel nothing, though you see nothing, even though it seems impossible to you. It is in dryness and in barrenness, in sickness and in feebleness that your prayer is most pleasing to me, even though you think that it has little savor for you.[2]

At this stage one has moved away from concern with doing. One is content to be. Such being is, of course, more than drowsy indolence or daydreaming. It is a moment in which all one's energies are concentrated in a single intense stream – like a laser. Far from being insulated from the immediate environment – drugged out of reality by religion, as it were – there is a high degree of personal presence to concrete existence. This is why the saints interacted so creatively with the world in which they lived. The contemplative is one who is progressively more attached to the ascended Christ, present throughout the universe. As such he or she becomes a channel through which the power of the risen Lord can reach out to heal what is amiss.

In a certain sense the contemplative act is like stepping out of space and time. The inner space and duration of such experiences have no relation with the spatio-temporal shell in which they occur. There is a concentrated awareness of the totality of our experiences – including those we would rather forget – though these are not the object of our attention but, as it were, the matrix by which the experience is shaped. We are not looking at ourselves, but are yet aware that every atom of our historical being is involved in the encounter toward which we are moving.

When we step outside space-time, we step inside God. We view God from within, as it were – not as an object outside ourselves. Relationship has become intimacy; intimacy has become identification – so the mystics tell us. Because our whole being is a participation in the being of God, when we become fully present to our essential selves we discover that to live means to move deeper into the Mystery of God. Of us it can be said that we, also, are "toward God." Still on earth, still involved with persons and projects, still manifestly imperfect, yet relentlessly on the move toward God.

Another way of expressing this supreme paradox is to say that in contemplative prayer God ceases to be the object of our prayer, but becomes its subject. The one who prays in us. Alternatively our prayer can be conceived as our participation in the prayer of Christ. Having the mind of Christ, to use Saint Paul's phrase (1 Corinthians 2:16, Philippians 2:5), means that we enter into Christ's subjectivity. So conformed is our will to his that when we say "I" we mean "Christ." "I live now not I, but Christ lives in me" (Galatians 2:20; see Philippians 1:21). When we gaze toward the Father, we see through

Christ's eyes. Our attitudes to human beings are imprinted with those of Christ: compassion, understanding, self-offering. In a mysterious way we become most fully ourselves by "putting on Christ" (Galatians 3:27, Romans 13:14).

Such prayer can become more Trinitarian as time goes on. Prayer assumes different emphases. There are occasions in which one is more powerfully aware of being drawn toward the Father: desire, aspiration, a stretching forth at the level of being. At other times one is more aware of the impulsion of the Holy Spirit; one is possessed by a force and a love not one's own that pushes one beyond normal limits. It is the Spirit that spans the chasm between us and the Father (Romans 8:26) and teaches us to call out *Abba* (Galatians 4:5–6, Romans 8:15). Most often, perhaps, our experience of prayer seems centered on identification or solidarity with Jesus the Word or, in a wider sense, it is experienced as communion with the Church, with the saints, with the Mother of the Lord, with all humanity – even with the cosmos. These experiences can coincide, for they are not mutually exclusive, but it is normal for one or other to claim precedence at different times in our life.

Such prayer, grounded as it is in truth, has a curiously refreshing character about it. Stepping back from the tyranny of time renews youthfulness (Psalm 103:5, Isaiah 40:31) and helps us regain that character of childlike simplicity that was so favored by Jesus (Mark 10:14–15). At the other end of the scale, contemplation gives a wisdom that surpasses age or experience, as is demonstrated in the biblical examples of Samuel and Daniel and others.

In the Book of Revelation the risen Lord is presented as the renewer and restorer of creation (Revelation 21:5). "If anyone is in Christ, a new creation takes place" (2 Corinthians 5:17, see Galatians 6:15). "We are as newborn babes" (2 Peter 2:2). Our transparency is restored and we begin to reflect the likeness of God in whose image we were created. In some mysterious way the expectation of the whole created order has been realized.

This dark encounter with God returns us to the innocence lost when the gates of Eden slammed behind us: not merely to the guileless incapacity for evil that we see in children but to a sage and stable preference for what is good and true. Knowing good and evil, by the power of God's grace we opt for good so radically that any previous wavering is set at nought. Happy are those who see God, for they shall become clean of heart! This paradoxical restoration explains why God is described in one of the ancient collects of the Roman liturgy as "the lover and restorer of innocence." How illogical! Innocence is such that its charm consists in never having been lost. Once squandered it is impossible to recover. Yes, God's action is illogical. In fact illogicality and impossibility are the hallmarks of divine intervention (Genesis 18:14, Luke 1:37). In contemplative prayer the innocence that we have lost is given back to us intact. Our sins are remitted. Not merely overlooked, ignored, excused or even forgiven but entirely negated. God's act of salvation transcends time. The damage we have inflicted on ourselves is neutralized. This is truly regeneration; no signs of our former degeneracy remain. In the contemplative experience we realize in fact the potential inherent in baptism. Another way of saying the same thing: the communion brought about in the Eucharist reaches its climax in contemplation. Between our initiation into God and its culmination there *seems* to be a delay while the residues of sin are burnt out and the fires of charity are fanned into flame. However this impression owes more to the distortion brought about by our perception of time than to the reality of God's act. God's definitive saving of us needs to be described in the present tense. God is eternally creating us, conserving us, redeeming us; if we perceive this then we can know that the Spirit is working within us. Our efforts to live a "spiritual life" simply confirm that this is so.

Contemplative prayer is certainly the summit of Christian life, it is the goal to which we all tend. This is the blessedness of eternal life for which we were created and which is *sometimes* given to us to experience here below. Contemplative prayer is the ordinary outcome of a life of fidelity to basic Christian imperatives; it operates even when the person is unaware of the gift received. Many simple persons of faith frequent this sanctuary without knowing the name of what they experience.

There is nothing exclusive about it – except that it seems reserved to the small and humble, to those who do not deserve it. There is certainly nothing flashy about contemplation: there is nothing in it that can be translated into marketable commodities and subsequently traded for some temporal advantage. Contemplation is entirely gratuitous, pure grace. On God's part total gift, on ours total receptivity. The Word became flesh to be with us. He called us to join him so that we might, together with the whole human family, consecrate our lives to this lifelong journey that carries us toward God.

APPENDIX

The Western Tradition
of Prayer

The sonorous subtitle of this book may seem unsuitable for such a frankly personal approach to prayer. Typically I remain unrepentant. It is true, this is not a systematic study of Western mysticism such as Cuthbert Butler undertook half a century ago. It is also true that its sources are limited: there is scant reference to anything after the fourteenth century. The Victorines are absent. The Rhenish and Flemish mystics are not represented, and the list of important writers on prayer and contemplation who are not mentioned is large.

Still I believe the subtitle accurate. Tradition is not a fixed body of doctrine. Rather it is a stream of beliefs, values and practices with a certain continuity of language and image – and a continuous rejuvenation of the present by the past. Whatever I believe and cherish about prayer comes from the ethos of Cistercian and Benedictine monasticism in which I have been immersed for most of my adult life. I have had some contact with the Christian East, and with the religions and traditions of East Asia; but my fundamental formation in prayer is Western. In no way do I consider myself to have mastered such vast and profound wisdom, but I have exercised myself constantly in it these past decades. My own philosophy of prayer is quite inseparable from it.

A composer of music unconsciously re-expresses the kind of music he or she personally enjoys. I suppose the same must be true in every sphere of endeavor. What follows is a list of some of my favorite Western authors – revealing something of the background from which I write. A reader who finds my approach attractive will find here some indications toward further reading. In the course of this book I have quoted from these authors, allowing them to speak for themselves and giving an idea of the magisterial way in which they approach deep matters. These quotations could be multiplied. May this listing be a token of my profound indebtedness.

1. Saint John Cassian (360–435)

Cassian, who founded twin monasteries near Marseilles, was instrumental in making available to Western monks the teachings of the Desert Fathers, and at least some of the psychological and philosophical expertise of Evagrius Ponticus. His teaching on prayer is contained in two conferences attributed to Abba Isaac *(Conferences 9 & 10)*, although supporting doctrine is scattered throughout his writing. Although, to my knowledge, there is no complete translation of Cassian in modern English, his two conferences on prayer are available in at least three versions.

2. Saint Augustine of Hippo (354–430)

Saint Augustine is perhaps the most towering intellectual figure in the development of Latin Christianity. His works are vast; I have met no one who has read them all, even cursorily. Augustine's spiritual doctrine is both delicate and profound. It is found less in his theological tractates and polemical works, but mostly in his sermons and biblical commentaries. The works I have read most closely include the *Confessions* (of course), *Tractates on the Gospel of John*, *Tractates on the Epistle of John*, his sermons and commentaries *On the Psalms*, and various other segments. Augustine can be exasperating at times, though he has the capacity to transform a boring passage with a sudden change of mood and an incisive phrase. He is strongest when he speaks out of his own rich experience; when he begins to talk about out-there theology, something is lost.

3. Saint Benedict of Nursia (480–547)

Saint Benedict was not much of a writer; his only literary bequest was his Rule for monasteries – and that was a scissors and paste job done on an earlier Italian rule. His genius lay in setting up a monastic organization solid enough to withstand the barbarians and the Dark Ages, yet flexible enough to adapt to changing circumstances in the centuries that followed. Many of the best qualities of Western spirituality can be (loosely) termed Benedictine: moderation, practicality, emphasis on the nexus between behavior and prayer, the importance of the liturgy, the quality of humanity. Benedict was a product of the West, but he personally contributed much, in a non-literary way, to the evolution of Western spirituality.

4. Saint Gregory the Great (540–604)

Gregory was a monk who became bishop of Rome. He is reputed to have written the biography of St Benedict, and was strongly influenced by both Augustine and Cassian. His principal work on the contemplative life is his commentary *On Ezekiel*. But there is a vast volume of spiritual teaching to be had also in his *Gospel Homilies*, his *Moral Commentary of the Book of Job* and in his *Pastoral Rule*. Gregory is not very original and his style is a little wooden, but there is a great deal of nourishment to be found in his works. He was certainly influential for later Western tradition.

5. Saint Bernard of Clairvaux (1090–1153)

Bernard was the product of at least six centuries of Latin tradition, which he absorbed and re-expressed with a brilliance and verve that are, at times, astonishing. A man of experience, spirituality and great personal depth, he expressed himself succinctly and often unconventionally on prayer and spiritual experience. He is often badly served by his admirers and imitators, and is extremely difficult to translate. Around Bernard could be clustered other great figures of the Cistercian century – William of St Thierry, Aelred of Rievaulx, Isaac of Stella, Guerric of Igny and others. One should also mention the great women mystics of the following century, especially the amazing Gertrude of Helfta.

6. *The Cloud of Unknowing*

There is a special charm about the fourteenth-century mystics of England, because they wrote in our own language. The author of *The Cloud of Unknowing* is unknown; but this work and other treatises on the contemplative life are a marvelous compendium of spiritual teaching in the West.

7. Julian of Norwich (1343–1416)

The book of *Showings* of the anchoress Julian is one of the most beautiful and profound spiritual works ever written. Saturated with an attractive blend of common sense and a deep understanding of theological truth, Julian's writings have great power to move and encourage a modern reader.

An extensive account of monastic spirituality conceived from the perspective of the study of the Bible can be found in my book: *Sacred Reading: The Ancient Art of Lectio Divina*, Triumph, Liguori, MO, 1996.

For those who wish to pursue themes and issues raised in the course of this book a recently published collection of my articles may give more detailed information: *The Undivided Heart: The Western Monastic Approach to Contemplation*, St. Bede's Publications, Petersham, MA, 1994.

I have also written an overview on "Western (Latin) Spirituality," in Michael Downey (ed.), *The New Dictionary of Catholic Spirituality*, Liturgical Press, Collegeville, MN, 1993; pp. 1021–1027.

NOTES

Abbreviations

CChr   *Corpus Christianorum,* Series Latina, Brepols, Turnhout, 1954–.

PL   *Patrologia Latina,* ed. J. P. Migne, Editions Garnier, Paris, 1844–55.

RB   *The Rule of Saint Benedict.* Various editions and translations available.

SBO   *Sancti Bernardi Opera,* Editions Cistercienses, Rome, 1957–.

SChr   *Sources Chrétiennes,* Cerf, Paris, 1942–.

Chapter 1

1. Cf. Augustine of Hippo, *Commentary on the Psalms* 49.7; CChr 38, p. 581. The same image occurs in Bernard of Clairvaux, *Parable* 7; SBO 6b.296.8.

Chapter 2

1. Gregory the Great, *Moral Commentary on the Book of Job* 23:47; PL 76, 279d–280a.

Chapter 3

1. Bernard of Clairvaux, *Sermons on the Song of Songs* 18.6; SBO 1.107.26–29.

2. William of St Thierry, *On the Song of Songs* 66; SChr 82, p. 166.

3. *The Cloud of Unknowing* ch. 4; pp. 18–19. In the first edition of this work I left the quotations from *The Cloud of Unknowing* and Julian of Norwich fairly close to the Middle English original. It was brought to my attention that this caused difficulty for some readers. In this revised edition I have modernized the text more, while attempting to keep to the rhythm and vocabulary of the originals. The page numbers refer to the critical edition by Phyllis Hodgson, *The Cloud of Unknowing and the Book of Privy Counselling,* published for the Early English Text Society by Oxford University Press, 1944.

4. *The Cloud of Unknowing,* ch. 34; p. 70.

Chapter 4

1. Quoted in Cassian, *Conference* 9.31; SChr 54, p. 66.

2. [The author of *The Cloud of Unknowing*], *A Pistle of Discrecioun of Stirings,* edited by Phyllis Hodgson in *Deonise Hid Divinite and Other Treatises on Contemplative Prayer related to The Cloud of Unknowing,*

published for the Early English Text Society by Oxford University Press, 1958. The quotation is from p. 69.

3. Bernard of Clairvaux, *Sermons on the Song of Songs* 56.7; *SBO* 2.118.16–18.

4. Gregory the Great, *Dialogues* 3.34.2; *SChr* 260, p. 400.

5. John Cassian, *Conference* 9.26; *SChr* 54, p.62.

6. John Cassian, *Conference* 9.27; *SChr* 54, p. 63.

Chapter 5

1. *The Cloud of Unknowing*, ch. 4; p. 20.

2. Dom Roger Hudleston (ed.), *The Spiritual Letters of Dom John Chapman* O.S.B., Sheed and Ward, London, 1935; letter 12, p. 53.

3. Gregory the Great, *Gospel Homily* 36.1; *PL* 76; col. 1266.

4. Gregory the Great, *Gospel Homily* 25.2; *PL* 76; col. 1191a.

5. *Didache* 8.

Chapter 6

1. John Cassian, *Conference* 9.8; *SChr* 54, pp. 48–49.

2. Hudleston, *op. cit.*, Introduction, p. 25.

3. *The Cloud of Unknowing*, ch. 14; p. 42.

4. Athanasius of Alexandria, *A Letter to Marcellinus* 12; this letter has been translated by R. Gregg in the Classics of Western Spirituality series, Paulist Press, New York, 1980; cf. p. 111.

Chapter 7

1. *The Cloud of Unknowing*, ch. 31; p. 66.

2. *The Cloud of Unknowing*, ch. 32; p. 66.

3. Caesarius of Arles included among the sermons of Augustine of Hippo, 300.2; *PL* 39, col. 2319c.

4. Augustine of Hippo, *Commentary on the Psalms* 49.1; *CChr* 38, p. 575.

Chapter 8

1. William of St Thierry, *Golden Epistle* 122; *SChr* 223, p. 240.

2. In the course of the 1983 Templeton Address, Solzhenitsyn observed: "And if I were called upon to identify briefly the principal trait of the *entire* twentieth century, here too, I would be unable to find anything more precise and pithy than to repeat once again: 'Men have forgotten God'. The failings

of human consciousness, deprived of its divine dimension, have been a determining factor in all the major crimes of this century." *The Orthodox Monitor*, 15 (January to July 1983), p. 3.

3. Basil of Caesarea, *Small Asceticon* 2; *PL* 103, col. 492b.

Chapter 9

1. Some of the relevant parts of Cyprian's treatise *On the Lord's Prayer* (PL 4, col. 535–562) can be found in the Office of Readings in the *Roman Breviary* for Week 11 of Ordinary Time.

2. *RB* 52.4.

3. *RB* 18.3.

4. *The Cloud of Unknowing*, ch. 7; pp. 28–29.

5. John Cassian, *Conference* 10.10; *SChr* 54, pp. 89–90.

6. John Cassian, *Institutes* 10.3; *SChr* 109, p. 76.

7. *The Cloud of Unknowing*, ch. 46; p. 86.

8. Cf. John Cassian, *Conference* 10.11; *SChr* 54, pp. 90–91.

9. John Cassian, *Institutes* 2.11.2; *SChr* 109, pp. 77–78.

10. *The Cloud of Unknowing*, ch. 35; p. 71.

11. John Cassian, *Conference* 1.22; *SChr* 42, p. 107.

12. Quoted in Gerhard Ebeling, *On Prayer: Nine Sermons* (The Preacher's Paperback Library), The Fortress Press, Philadelphia, 1966; p. 46.

Chapter 10

1. *The Cloud of Unknowing*, ch. 70; p. 124.

2. *The Cloud of Unknowing*, ch. 68; pp. 121–122.

3. *The Cloud of Unknowing*, ch. 41; p. 80.

4. John Cassian, *Conference* 9.3; *SChr* 54, p. 42.

5. John Cassian, *Conference* 9.20; *SChr* 54, pp. 57–58.

6. Bernard of Clairvaux, *Sermons on the Song of Songs* 11.12; *SBO* 1.55. 12–19.

7. [The author of *The Cloud of Unknowing*], *The Book of Privy Counselling*, (same volume), p. 152.

8. John Cassian, *Conference* 9.3; *SChr* 54, pp. 42–43.

Chapter 11

1. Gregory the Great, *Moral Commentary on the Book of Job* 23.43; *PL* 76, col. 277–278.

2. Bernard of Clairvaux, *Sermons on the Song of Songs* 17.2; *SBO* 1.99. 12–21.

3. *The Cloud of Unknowing*, ch. 75; pp. 131–132.

4. Augustine of Hippo, *On the Psalms* 50.24; *CChr* 38, p. 615.

5. Bernard of Clairvaux, *Sermons on the Song of Songs* 18.3; *SBO* 2.299. 21–29.

6. Bernard of Clairvaux, *Sermons on the Song of Songs* 74.5–7; *SBO* 2.242–244; I have abridged the section and have changed the order of some paragraphs.

7. Bernard of Clairvaux, *Sermons on the Song of Songs* 85.13; *SBO* 2.315–316.

8. Bernard of Clairvaux, *Sermons on the Song of Songs* 85.13; *SBO* 2.316.8.

9. [The author of *The Cloud of Unknowing*], *A Tretyse of the Stodye of Wysdome that Men Clepen Beniamyn*, in *Deonise Hid Divinite*, p. 42.

10. Gregory the Great, *Gospel Homilies* 25.2; *PL* 76, col. 1191a.

11. Gregory the Great, *Gospel Homilies* 27.1; *PL* 76, col. 1275a.

Chapter 13

1. Augustine of Hippo, *On the Psalms* 29/2.1; *CChr* 38, p. 174.

2. Edmund Colledge and James Walsh (ed.), *A Book of Showings to the Anchoress Julian of Norwich*, Pontifical Institute of Mediaeval Studies, Toronto, 1978; chapter 61, revelation 14; pp. 602–603.

3. *Id.*, chapter 48, revelation 14; pp. 501–2.

4. Augustine of Hippo, *On the Psalms* 50.20; *CChr* 38, p. 614.

5. Augustine of Hippo, *On the Psalms* 55.13; *CChr* 39, p. 687.

6. Augustine of Hippo, *On the Psalms* 50.15; *CChr* 38, p. 611.

7. Augustine of Hippo, *Tractates on the Gospel of John* 18.10; *CChr* 36, p. 186.

8. Augustine of Hippo, *On the Psalms* 56.7; *CChr* 39, p. 698.

9. *The Cloud of Unknowing*, ch. 16; p. 44.

10. Bernard of Clairvaux, *Sermons on the Song of Songs* 83.1; *SBO* 2.298–299.

Chapter 14

1. Thomas Merton, *The Climate of Monastic Prayer* (CS 1), Cistercian Publications, Spencer, 1970; p. 121. See also my article, "Thomas Merton's Notes on 'Inner Experience' Twenty Five Years Afterwards," *Tjurunga* 44 (1993), pp. 30–55.

2. *Revelations*, 14.41; pp. 464–465.

ABOUT THE AUTHOR

Michael Casey, O.C.S.O., is a Cistercian monk of Tarrawarra Abbey in Yarra Glen, Australia. He is well-known as a retreat master and lecturer on monastic spirituality. He holds a doctorate from Melbourne College of Divinity in the area of the life and writings of St. Bernard of Clairvaux.

He is the author of The Undivided Heart: *The Western Monastic Approach to Contemplation*, published by St. Bede's Publications, and *Sacred Reading: The Ancient Art of Lectio Divina*, published by Triumph Books.